Educating for democracy
HORACE MANN

Britannica Bookshelf—Great Lives for Young Americans

Educating for democracy

HORACE MANN

by Jessie Treichler

Illustrated by Robert Boehmer

Published by
ENCYCLOPAEDIA BRITANNICA PRESS, *Chicago*

For Paul and Paula

Copyright © 1962 by Encyclopaedia Britannica
Library of Congress Catalog Number 62-10426
Printed in the United States of America

Copyright under International Copyright Union
All Rights Reserved under Pan American and Universal Copyright Conventions

TABLE OF CONTENTS

Chapter 1

Two Pieces of Advice

Horace Mann pushed back the journal book he had been writing in and closed his eyes with relief. He had made up his mind. He had just written:

> June 29, 1837: The chance of being offered a station which would change the whole course of my action, and consequently of my duties, through life, was not to be regarded with indifference. The deep feeling of interest was heightened by the reflection, that, in case of my receiving the appointment of Secretary of the Board of Education, my sphere of *possible* usefulness would be indefinitely enlarged, and that my failure would forever force into contrast the noble duty and the inadequate discharge of it. The day is past. I have received the offer. The path of usefulness is opened before me. My present purpose is to enter into it. Few undertakings, according to my appreciation of it, have been greater. I know of none which may be more fruitful in beneficient results. God grant me an annihilation of selfishness, a mind of wisdom, a heart of benevolence.

The path of usefulness is opened before me.

At 41, Horace Mann knew that he stood where two paths diverged. To this point, he had in his own life walked, step by step, the journey from ignorance to knowledge. He would never forget the cold, the hunger, the long hours of toil as a boy on a New England farm. He would never forget the nights of terror and agony that the ignorant suffer from bigotry. He would never have to look farther than his own yearning struggle to become educated to see what education meant.

He had become a successful lawyer, and had been successively elected Town Moderator of Dedham, Massachusetts;

State Representative in the Massachusetts Legislature for the Dedham district; State Senator from Boston; and finally President of the Senate. In that last office, he had signed into law a bill creating the first state Board of Education in the United States. The Board was to report annually to the Legislature on the condition of the public schools of Massachusetts and to recommend changes that would give the children of Massachusetts the best education possible.

As Secretary of the Board, Horace Mann would have the task of collecting information, informing the people of the best educational methods available, and preparing the Board's Annual Report. Compared to the prospects afforded him by his combination of brilliant legal and oratorical skill and his solid base of political success, the Secretaryship was a mere clerk's job, Mann's friends told him, where he would be underpaid and overworked. Yet Horace had chosen the Secretaryship.

A century and a quarter later, Horace Mann would be known as the "Father of the American Public School." Schools would be named for him, not only throughout the United States but all over the world. This is the story of what led Horace Mann to his crucial and difficult decision, and what he did on the "path of usefulness."

Horace Mann was born in Franklin, Massachusetts, on Wednesday, May 4, 1796. Later, he was to observe ruefully, that the old nursery rhyme had characterized Monday's child as fair of face, Tuesday's child as full of grace, but Wednesday's child as full of woe.

Mann lived and worked in unsettled, tumultuous, changing, hopeful times, the years that saw the United States,

20 years old at his birth, grow toward maturity.

Franklin was a country village, but it was only 20 miles from Boston, about 20 miles from Providence, Rhode Island, and 20 miles from Quincy, Massachusetts, the home of such history-makers as Samuel, John, and John Quincy Adams. Franklin stood high among the towns of the vicinity for intelligence, morality, and worth. The citizens of Franklin were not uninformed country bumpkins. Its older men had fought in the American Revolution; its young people grew up knowing them; and they all knew, at least in part, what Jefferson had meant when he wrote, "We hold these truths to be self-evident, that all men are created equal, that they are endowed by their Creator with certain inalienable Rights, that among these are Life, Liberty, and the pursuit of Happiness." At least they could agree that as American citizens they had the rights to life and liberty. As New Englanders brought up in strict Calvinistic tradition, however, they may well have questioned "the pursuit of Happiness."

The people of Franklin took great delight in talking everything over. They questioned travelers about news of the day, and discussed what they had heard. They talked over letters that came about such stirring events as the Louisiana Purchase and the burning of Washington in the War of 1812. The village store, the smithy, the post office, and the tavern were centers for discussion. But the one center that drew all together—children as well as their parents—was the parish church, where everyone in Franklin attended two church services every Sunday.

Thomas and Rebecca Stanley Mann, Horace's parents, had been married in 1786 in the unsettled days after the Revolution. Their home was about half a mile from Franklin, on a piece of land known as Mann's Plain, which had been cleared from the forest 67 years before by Thomas's grandfather. Thomas was fifth in descent from William Mann, who had come to Massachusetts Bay in the 17th century. Horace was the fourth of five children of Thomas and Rebecca Mann. When Horace was born, his sister Rebecca was nine, Thomas Stanley was eight, and Stephen was four; Lydia was born two years later.

Thomas Mann was a small farmer, one of the plain people of the Commonwealth of Massachusetts. The whole family had to work hard to make ends meet. Horace said later, "I believe in the rugged nursing of Toil; but she nursed me too much. In the winter time in in-door and sedentary occupations, which confined me too strictly; and in summer, when I could work on the farm, the labor was too severe, and often encroached upon the hours of sleep. I do not remember the time when I began to work. Even my play-days—not play-days, for I never had any, but my play-hours—were earned by extra exertion, finishing tasks early to gain a little leisure for boyish sports."

Nothing indicates that Horace's childhood differed much from that of most New England children in those days. The house the Manns lived in was a two-story, frame one, very good for the time and place. His parents were respected, even loved, in Franklin. Thomas Mann neither did nor spoke evil, and he taught his sons to earn their way as they went, not to borrow against expectations. Rebecca Mann, Horace's mother, was an extraordinary woman. She had excellent intellect and intuition, if not education, and was completely devoted to her children. Her direction and guidance were strong upon Horace, and he had the most profound respect and affection for her throughout all his life.

At the same time, a reserve existed between Horace and his parents—as must have existed between most parents and children of the time—and that reserve made it impossible to speak to them freely about the thoughts and emotions that troubled him most gravely, or even about his health.

The reasons for the difference in Horace's reaction to his childhood from that of other children of his time lay partly in his sensitive and grave temperament; partly in his health, which was never robust; and partly in his craving for education, which could never be appeased. To be endlessly bound to the toil of the farm and to lack the time and money for learning were undoubtedly torment to this boy.

At the same time, however, that Horace recorded in later years his rebellion at the never-ending toil and privations of his youth, he noted that although his parents had not had the means to give him knowledge, they had intensified his love for it. "They always spoke of learning and learned men with enthusiasm and a kind of reverence. I was taught to take care of the books we had, as though there was something sacred about them." After he became famous, his sister Lydia wrote him that his devotion to education, his pleading for the slave, his temperance principles, and his sympathy with the wretched and miserable, all could be traced to the parental home. He never forgot his childhood feeling of being oppressed, nor his craving for the education that he then felt would be forever denied him.

Until Horace was 15 years old, he never attended school more than eight or ten weeks a year. Usually, during the winter months the Mann children attended the local district school; but Horace sometimes walked four miles to the Williams Academy in Wrentham to get a few more weeks of schooling after the district school had closed.

The era of the district schools, supported solely by taxes raised by the districts, is regarded as one of the most depressing in the educational history of the United States. It is not a time one would want to see repeated. Small and poor districts had small and poor schools. Children had to buy their own school books. Horace Mann braided straw for hats made in a neighboring factory to pay for his. The master, frequently chosen in town meeting, was usually some young man principally interested in raising some money to advance his own education, or some young woman who wanted to raise a little additional money for her hope chest. There was no central control, no organized and uniform course of study. The master could teach anything he wanted to teach, so long as it did not offend the religious convictions of the community. He could leave untaught anything he did not want to teach—or did not know enough about. These teachers, Horace Mann observed later, were "very good people . . . but very poor teachers."

The school building in Franklin was typical of those of the poorer districts. It was small, unpainted, weatherbeaten, with primitive ventilation. A wide-throated chimney provided children sitting near it with almost tropical heat, but ten feet from the fireplace, the temperature was arctic. In winter, ink froze in the inkwells. Then, though ideas might flow, they could not be put on paper.

Memory was highly prized and greatly rewarded in the Franklin schools; independent thought and investigation—anything even loosely resembling the creative—was frowned upon. In fact, it was not only frowned upon but frequently

[*13*]

punished. There was little appeal to the imagination, and all sense of beauty and the freshness of vision of childhood were discouraged. Children with a sense of the poetic, a love for the beautiful, a passion for color had no place to turn. One of Horace's bitterest complaints in later life was that his first teachers had insisted that his eyes be turned always to books —which were without illustrations except of the crudest kind —and not to beauty and its expression in nature and the fine arts. He was never taught, he said, to distinguish the forms and colors of Nature all around him. "Our ears were strangers to music. So far from being taught the art of drawing, which is a beautiful language in itself, I well remember that when the impulse to express in pictures what I could not express in words was so strong that . . . it tingled down to my fingers, then my knuckles were rapped with the heavy ruler of the teacher, or cut with his rod, so that an artificial tingling soon drove away the natural."

This could have been the complaint of the unhappy child who believed that he had more ability than he actually had. It could have been the whine of the child without ability who felt he was not appreciated. In later years, however, after Horace Mann had won and developed normal schools for the training of good teachers, the pupils he thus freed—literally "created"—proved that he had been only just in his criticism.

Franklin had a small but rather good library. The village, once called Wrentham, West Precinct, was incorporated as a town in 1778, and named for Benjamin Franklin, who had just secured an important alliance with France. His reputation was at its height. Various towns and counties in the United States hurried to take his name as their own, not so much to honor him as to honor themselves. It was suggested to Franklin that he give the newly named village a bell for the new church steeple, but "sense being preferable to sound," he said, he decided to give books instead. He asked a friend "to make a choice of proper books to commence a library for the Inhabitants of Franklin" to the value of £25.

With this gift as its base, an independent library association was formed in the village, to which each member paid $1 a year for the privilege of using the books. Thomas Mann was a member. By the time Horace could read, the association was on a firm enough footing so that every citizen in the community could use the library. It contained a great many sermons, but it also had works by Joseph Addison, Alexander Pope, and other standard English writers, as well as some good history and fiction. Here undoubtedly Horace was introduced to history, government, and economics. Memories of this library moved him to say later, and passionately, that, had he the power, he would scatter libraries over the land as the farmer sows his wheat field with seed. Probably the Franklin Library more than anything else decided Horace to try to get good basic libraries for the public schools.

A final educational influence on young Horace Mann was the parish church. Dr. Nathaniel Emmons had been the pastor in Franklin since 1775. Not only did he preach to the entire population of Franklin twice each Sunday, but he ruled the congregation with an iron hand for more than 50 years. It is difficult today to realize the hold that Calvinism— and Dr. Emmons was a super-Calvinist—had upon New England at this period, and was to have for many years to come.

At no other place in the world except Scotland and Puritan England had the grip of Calvinism ever been so tight. Essentially, the dominant idea of Calvinism is the infinite rule of God. While God is the source of all good, man is guilty and corrupt. To the Calvinists the first man was made in the image of God, which meant that he was pure and all things good. Because of Adam's fall in the Garden of Eden, all later men became depraved and corrupted. Even though a man might lead a good and blameless life, he still bore the curse of Adam's sin. Thus, all men were depraved and corrupt. Only God could determine who should be saved, and no man could save himself by goodness and piety.

Dr. Emmons spared no pains to bring before his congregation the most intimate knowledge of the severest doctrines of his creed. By the time Horace was ten years old, he knew Calvinism well. Because he was at once realistic and imaginative, he took much of what he heard from the pulpit literally. He was himself tortured at night imagining the tortures of those who, through no fault of their own, were eternally damned to suffering. Many of them, he realized, could be people he loved most. Although Horace's parents were sensible people, they were also people of their time. They listened to Dr. Emmons, and they feared God. They could probably not have eased Horace's fears even if he could have brought himself to tell them of his tortured thoughts.

On June 20, 1809, when Horace was 13, Thomas Mann died of tuberculosis. Thomas's health had been poor for many years, and his death was probably not unexpected. His will provided that about $200 go to each of his children when they came of age. The farm was to be managed by his oldest son, Thomas Stanley—known as Stanley—and was to be the home of Mrs. Mann so long as she should remain his widow.

[*16*]

The Mann family, following the death of Thomas, indeed fell on hard times, although they had always lived close to the bone. Stanley was an easier taskmaster than his father had been, but poverty is the harshest taskmaster of all. There was heavy work to do in the fields and in keeping up the farm. There was endless spinning, and endless weaving. There was endless braiding of straw for hats, work which gave the family almost the only outside income it had. Horace was not adept at straw-braiding, and became very impatient with the tiresome task. His sister Lydia, whom he taught to read and write, marveled that he could be so patient as a teacher when he was so impatient with the job of braiding straw.

In later years, Mann wrote to a friend that he would give him "two pieces of advice which shall be gratis to you though they cost me what is more valuable than diamonds. Train your children to work, though not too hard; and . . . let them sleep as much as they will. I have derived one compensation, however, from the rigor of my early lot. Industry or diligence became my second nature; and I think it would puzzle any psychologist to tell where it joined on to the first. Owing to these ingrained habits, work has always been to me what water is to the fish. . . . with me, whenever I had anything to do, I do not remember ever to have demurred, but have always set about to do it like a fatalist; and it was as sure to be done as the sun is to set."

A little over a year after Horace's father died, another blow fell on the family—one from which Horace Mann never wholly recovered. On July 22, 1810, on a Sunday, Stephen Mann at 17 was drowned in Uncas Pond, near Franklin. Although Stephen was greatly respected and liked, he had a kind of humor and even irreverence that, although much appreciated by his younger brother, probably were not much appreciated by Dr. Emmons. Also, Stephen had committed the capital sin of going swimming on Sunday. Dr. Emmons took advantage of the funeral sermon, not to give words of comfort to the grieving family, but to lecture the young people present on the dangers of dying unconverted. He dwelt on the probabilities of Stephen's soul being already in Hell's torment, and assured his listeners that those saved and in Paradise were rejoicing even now in such judgment as a part of God's wisdom. The sobbing of his mother, combined with his own grief and growing belief in a God of mercy, drove Horace from the ranks of Calvinism forever. Later in life he wrote, "What an unspeakable calamity a Calvinist education is! What a dreadful thing it was for me!"

Chapter **2**

The Happiest Years

Horace Mann was 20 years old when he met Samuel Barrett, a traveling schoolmaster, who came into the district and opened a school. His fees were low enough for Horace to afford them. His qualifications were such that Horace yearned to study under him. He enrolled in Barrett's school.

The relationship between an able teacher and an eager pupil is unlike any other relationship in the world. It was said that Barrett was completely ignorant of some subjects. But he was a master of the Greek and Latin classics, and Horace took fire from his teaching. Some years before a young woman who had studied Latin had visited the Mann home. Horace had looked on her as a sort of goddess. He had read many of the classics in translation and knew them by heart in English. Now, the idea that he too could study them in the original languages broke upon his mind "with the wonder and bewilderment of a revelation."

Barrett has been described as an eccentric genius, full to overflowing with the classics, which he could quote by the page. It was said that he would keep school for six months, living and working in great sobriety, and then burst into a drunken frenzy that would last for the rest of the year.

Whatever Barrett was, he was obviously of higher calibre than the masters Horace Mann had previously worked under, and he was obviously the teacher for whom Horace had been waiting. Together, in six months, they covered many works unknown to most students today but then considered necessary for an educated man: Aesop's *Fables*; Virgil's *Aeneid,* and parts of his *Georgics* and *Bucolics*; Cicero's select orations; and in the New Testament, the four Gospels and parts of the Epistles in Greek.

Barrett, Horace Mann later said, never took a grammar or textbook into his hand, but quoted from memory. He would have considered it an indignity to have a pupil offer him a textbook for assigning the next lesson because his memory was so accurate. His ability inspired Horace not only with respect and conceptions of excellence, but also with "an ardor for attainment, such as all the places and prizes ever bestowed, and a life of floggings into the bargain, would never have imparted." Whenever Mann encountered difficulties then or later, either in translation or otherwise, he said that all he had to do was to think how easy it all would have been for Barrett. This thought, he said, "seemed not only to invigorate my effort, but to give me an enlargement of power, so that I could return to the charge, and triumph."

During this same time, Horace was also studying mathematics. He kept a large notebook filled with problems of geometry. This book was not only a model of painstaking neatness; it also illustrated page-by-page Horace Mann's originality. He drew each problem in the fullest detail—to measure the length from the tip of a shadow to the steeple from which it was cast, he meticulously drew the building and its

[20]

steeple, and even adorned the steeple with a weathervane. He wrote neatly flowing headings for each of his chapters and sections, not just titles in the elegant script of the period, but adding small details and additional adornments from his own imagination.

In March of 1816, while Horace was in the midst of this great concentration of effort, his brother Stanley, who was certainly no scholar, wrote him from Bellingham, Massachusetts, where he had gone on business: "Brother, Ever anxious for your welfare and that of my friends, I want to give some advice to you now in particular. I wish to see you engaged in your studies, but am told that you are too much so. This perhaps is a case which not often occurs, and therefore ought to be treated with the greatest delicacy .Diligence is ever to be recommended but not in the extreme. Your health should be your greatest care. . . . I wish you think of these things, Brother Horace, and so should you live as you may wish you had." Horace paid no attention to the advice. After all, he would be 20 years old in May.

In describing his longing for an education at this time, Horace Mann later said to a friend, "I know not how it was: its motive never took the form of wealth or fame. It was rather an instinct which impelled toward knowledge, as that of a migratory bird is impelled northward in spring-time. All my boyish castles in the air had reference to doing something for the benefit of mankind. The early precepts of benevolence, inculcated upon me by my parents, flowed out in this direction; and I had a conviction that knowledge was my needed instrument."

By the end of six months of study with Barrett, Horace had acquired enough education to be admitted to the sophomore class at Brown University, which he entered in September, 1816. Going to college for Horace Mann was roughly akin to starting out by camel to the Peacock Throne, even though Providence was only 20 miles from home. It was natural for Horace to go to Brown. The people of Franklin traveled to Providence rather than to Boston, and all the young men from Franklin who had gone to college had gone to Brown. First called Rhode Island College, Brown University had been started in 1774. Freedom of thought was implanted there, a natural extension of the freedom of thought that Roger Williams had implanted in the Providence Plantation 138 years before. The founders of Brown had decided it should be a liberal institution, in which no religious tests were to be required, and where all members had free and absolute liberty of conscience. These principles, in a day when teaching was still done by the clergy and any man's religious beliefs were subject to scrutiny, were all the more remarkable. Wealthy young men of the day tended to go to Harvard or Yale; Brown kept its costs as low and its course of study as practical as possible in an attempt to attract the studious and earnest sons of farmers, artisans, and tradesmen.

Dr. Asa Messer, president of Brown since 1802, examined Horace for entrance and signed the receipt for $20 that Horace paid him to become a member of the sophomore class. Meals at the Commons cost Horace $1.89 a week; "Steward's services," $2.21 for the term; and sweeping down of the fireplace in his room—all rooms were heated thus—$1.17 for the year. Horace hoped that he could stretch his small inheritance over three years.

The happiest years Horace had known now lay before him. He was where he wanted to be. He had friends with similar tastes, interests, intellectual abilities, and ideals. He could now even regard his poverty with humor. In a letter to his sister, he said, "It is a long, long time since my last ninepence bade good-bye to its brethren; and I suspect the last two parted on no very friendly terms, for they have never since met together. Poor wretches! never did two souls stand in greater need of mutual support and consolation."

He felt some homesickness, too. He said that for several weeks past he had been in a "half-delirious state" because he had received no word from home.

He urged his sister to write, saying, "You seem to treat it as though it were a task, like the pilgrimage to Mecca, and to be performed but once in a lifetime. Perhaps you will say you have nothing to write about. Write about anything. . . . In your next letter, put in some sentences of mother's, just as she spoke them. . . . "

Horace soon took the first place in his class and in the college. He translated Greek and Latin authors with great facility, accuracy, "and elegance." He showed excellence in mathematics and astronomy. He was particularly able as a writer, debater, and orator.

There were two famous literary societies in Brown at the time, the Philermenians and the United Society of Brothers. These societies were composed of undergraduates who met together to debate and orate and to read their compositions to one another. To be chosen to either was an honor; and when Horace was invited during his first year to join the United Brothers, he was delighted. There was, however, a little matter of money. Dues were $3 during the freshman year, $2.50 for the sophomore and junior years, and $1 for seniors. Horace, always pressed for money but determined

[23]

not to lose his chance to join the United Brothers, worked out an arrangement whereby the Brothers used his room for Society meetings instead of charging him dues. The minutes of the meetings of the United Brothers were filled after this with the name of Horace Mann, and most of the members became his friends for life. During Horace's senior year, he was secretary of the Society, then vice-president and lecturer, and finally, president.

Horace Mann was a remarkably consistent and well organized person. Every step he took seemed, inevitably, to lead him to the next one, and always on a straight course. Everything he learned at one period of his life was put to use in the succeeding ones. At Brown he prepared essays and orations on topics which were to be of major importance to him in his later career: the separation of the church and state, freedom of the press, the place of the imagination in education, the uses of genius, and the study of mathematics.

In one essay, "Genius and Application," he wrote that genius without application promised much but accomplished little; while application without genius at first excited "almost disgust by its lingering tardiness, yet, at length, the unnoted advances of its slow but constant progress, fill us with pleasure and surprise."

In another essay, "To Improve Language Teaching," he said that it was the general nature of mankind to admire the splendid rather than the useful, and that he who pleased the imagination would gain the applause of more than he who enlightened the understanding. In his opinion, he remarked, there had been a monopoly of knowledge in America just as there had been a monopoly of wealth.

A notebook on English history was arranged with great

care and gave special attention to the growth of English liberty. Although he was always more interested in principles than in facts, his care in bringing together the historical facts for this notebook gave him a body of knowledge that he was to use again and again in later life, both as a lawyer and as an educator.

Ira M. Barton, who later became a judge, entered Brown in the sophomore class at the same time as Horace, and the two roomed together during their last two years. Judge Barton later recalled those days at Brown in language so seriously worded that he could have been addressing a jury: " . . . the dissipations of neither the college nor the city had any controlling attractions for us. During the three years of our college-life, I recollect not a single instance of impropriety on his part." His chum Horace, said Judge Barton, had qualities of such a high order that he attracted the attention and secured the respect, not only of members of their own class, but of members of the other classes as well. Their room was so much the center of good company that the Judge sometimes wished he had a less interesting and attractive roommate.

In letters home, Horace himself gave somewhat livelier accounts of those days. In one letter to Lydia, he said that since two students had recently been "rusticated," or suspended, and one expelled, he derived some hope for himself: "After a shower has passed over, we do not look for another so soon."

Ira Barton confessed that "one college sin, if sin it be deemed," was committed in their junior year. The students by tradition celebrated the Fourth of July with speeches in the chapel. In 1818, as punishment for some misdemeanor,

President Messer denied them the right to use the chapel. "A majority of the students went for resisting the government," Judge Barton said. "I went for loyalty. But my chum, being a little more impulsive, and having been chosen the orator for the occasion, went for independence and the celebration

The Brown boys celebrated Fourth of July independently.

of it. . . . I concluded, that, if there must be rebellion, I had better rebel against the college government than against the majority of my fellow-students. I took the front rank in the procession; helped to *open* the chapel door; and chum went in, and delivered his oration amidst great applause. A trifling fine was imposed upon him; but he lost no credit with either the students or the government."

Horace, writing home at the time to his family, said: "Finding that a place in the procession of the celebration in town had not been assigned to them, which they deemed sufficiently honorable" (they were to have been placed next to last in the parade line—just in front of "Strangers and Citizens"), they voted to celebrate by themselves and sent a committee to the President requesting permission to go into the chapel to hear an oration, but the request was denied. They determined, however, to go in and hazard the consequences, "peaceably if they could, forcibly if they must. . . . It was then expected that the door must be burst in, but in the morning this inscription was found upon it, written in Greek, 'And the door shall be opened unto you,' which was all done in its proper time (and which, by the way, I think to be a great verification of Scripture)." Following the reading of the Declaration of Independence, an appropriate prayer, and an oration in the Chapel, they then "repaired to the dining room where an excellent dinner was prepared for us and [we spent] the remainder of the day in hilarity and mirth."

In his senior year Horace was chosen to lead the United Brothers in a procession, and to take the "First Part," comparable to valedictorian, in his graduation ceremonies. His oration was "The Progressive Character of the Human Race," which was to be a favorite theme throughout his life. In his address he pictured a higher condition of human society when education would develop in people greater proportions of wisdom and virtue, when philanthropy would help take care of the wants and relieve the woes of man, and when free institutions would abolish the oppression of war.

Horace's glorious days at Brown were over. Although they occupied only three years of his life, they were three very important years. He was freed intellectually. He discovered that he was a natural leader. He enjoyed a rare companionship with young men of similar interests, some of whom became lifetime friends. He found his career.

In the early days of the 13 colonies, ministers had been the leaders of the nation. Following the Revolution, in the interpretation and execution of the law, lawyers became increasingly important. Wherever there is a free country, it must be based on law, for law is the base of all freedoms. With Horace's religious beliefs what they were, he could not have turned to the ministry. His natural bent and the advice of his teachers convinced him that he should become a lawyer. Accordingly, in mid-July, 1819, six weeks before the Brown Commencement, Mann entered the law office of Judge Josiah Fiske of Wrentham, Massachusetts.

He had been at his studies only until January of 1820, however, when he received a letter from Dr. Messer, President of Brown, inviting him to become a tutor at a salary of $350 a year.

Horace replied, saying that his greatest objection to accepting the offer arose "from a consciousness of inadequacy." But he admitted that insincere people talk this way and do not mean it. He accepted, adding as a postscript: "I have presumed that the consideration mentioned is to be exclusive of board."

Then he reconsidered and declined the offer. Dr. Messer wrote again. A month later, Horace again accepted the appointment, saying:

"It is with reluctance that I accept the appointment *when I consider* the arduous duties that will devolve upon me. My exertions, however, shall be directed to vindicate your responsibility in my appointment; and all that I can do is *to hope,* that my exertions may be so successful as to show that your confidence has not been too injudiciously misplaced."

No small part of the reasons for Horace's final acceptance must have been his need to earn some money and pay off his college debts. He was his father's son, and he did not want to live on expectations.

In September, 1820, Horace Mann took up his new duties at Brown University. However inadequate he may have felt when he began, Mann turned out to be an excellent teacher, one considerably in advance of his times. In his teaching of the Latin classics he combined study of the geography, biography, and history of the period with the study of the language itself, on the theory that it is easier to remember two or even ten associated ideas than one idea alone.

One day a student of Mann's asked the steward of the college what he was going to do with some medicinal preparation he had. "Mr. So and So," said the steward, "has a violent attack of fever, and I am going to give him a sweat."

"If you want to give him a sweat," said the student, "send him into Mr. Mann's recitation room without his lesson."

Both as an undergraduate and as a tutor, Horace Mann was a frequent and welcome visitor at President Messer's home. There were three Messer daughters—Mary, Caroline, and Charlotte—the youngest of whom became Horace's wife. Charlotte was only 12 when Horace was a tutor at Brown, but, as a contemporary wrote, he "carried her in his heart for the next ten years."

In spite of his success as a teacher and the pleasant company he found on the Brown campus, Horace continued to feel that law was his calling. He always felt the pressure of time; the thought that he would be 26 in May of 1822 probably determined him to return to the study of law as soon as possible.

In the spring of 1821 he wrote to friends studying at Litchfield, Connecticut for information about the school there, the first law school in the country. Their glowing reports determined him to go there. It took from 14 to 18 months to complete the course. Tuition was $100 for the first 12 months, and $60 for the remainder. Horace would probably have advanced standing because of his 13 months with Judge Fiske.

Welcome A. Burgess, who was graduated from Brown a year after Horace and was now at Litchfield, wrote Horace some advice: "Buy nothing in town. Owing to the excitement of a Religious Revival which is at present scarifying the town, they cheat ten times worse than usual."

Litchfield, Burgess went on to say, was indeed the place to make a lawyer: "Everything is legal and subordinate to the study of law. Law is the prevailing fashion. The minister will pray for you as the law directs. The merchant will cheat you as the law directs. The students will get drunk according to the precise letter of the statute in such case made and provided."

Horace took stock of his finances. He had saved something from his months of tutoring, and by selling the furnishings he had bought for his tutor's room at Brown—including a set of Homer—he thought he could manage Litchfield.

In February, 1822, he left Providence for Litchfield.

Chapter 3

Everything Is Legal

Litchfield, Connecticut, like many a New England town, was small, but large in its store of history and memories. In a workshop for the Continental Army there, the leaden statue of George III, erected in Bowling Green, New York, in 1770 and torn down by the citizens in 1776, was melted down to make bullets for the American army. Litchfield had been the birthplace of Ethan Allen, the conqueror of Fort Ticonderoga, and of Harriet Beecher Stowe, who wrote *Uncle Tom's Cabin*. From 1810 to 1826, Dr. Lyman Beecher, her father, preached fire and brimstone at the Litchfield First Congregational Church.

Inevitably, Horace Mann went to hear the famous Dr. Beecher. Mann himself was an authority on fire and brimstone from his boyhood years of listening to Dr. Emmons. Horace could not resist going to hear one of the greatest challengers to Satan of them all. He wrote his sister Lydia that he had never heard such a sermon in his life: "It produced as great an effect upon my feelings as it would have to have heard a great tragedy well performed at a theatre! *No more upon my belief;* for belief belongs to the understanding and should not be biased by hopes and fears."

Judge Tapping Reeve had opened the first law school in America in his Litchfield office in 1775. In 1784 he built a small schoolhouse in the yard near his house. In 1788, after he had been appointed Judge of the Superior Court of Connecticut, he took in James Gould as an associate in the law school. The school was never incorporated, its two small buildings were modest, and the lectures for the most part were conducted in the offices of its instructors. Yet, by the time the school closed in 1833, it had enrolled 1,024 students from every state in the Union. Of the students, 16 became United States Senators; 50, members of Congress, 40, judges of higher state courts; 8, chief justices of states; 10, governors of states; 5, cabinet officers; 2, justices of the United States Supreme Court; 1, Vice-president of the United States (John C. Calhoun); and several, foreign ministers.

At the time Horace Mann arrived in Litchfield, the school under Judge Gould was at the height of its reputation. The 30 or so students included Welcome Burgess, already Horace's friend from Brown, and Henry Augustus Rogers, another Brown graduate. Edward Greely Loring was there— a Harvard graduate from Boston. Horace occasionally called Loring "Glorious Neddy," perhaps with a bit of malice and even envy, since "Neddy" had the social position and money that Horace lacked. Edward Loring and Horace Mann later became law partners, and Loring became one of Horace's best and most steadfast friends.

J. W. Scott, another friend, later wrote that Horace was not only "the best fellow and the best wit" in the office, but also "the best whist player" in school. Scott met Horace for the first time in the room of James Sullivan of Boston, son of a famous and wealthy lawyer. James was confined to his room at the time with an eye infection, and Horace, always sympathetic with anyone who was ill, was reading the lessons in law aloud to James.

All in all, the law students at Litchfield were a serious and able group of young men, who felt the honor of being admitted to the school and were prepared to take advantage of every opportunity.

Not all the opportunities were in the office or the classroom. Between the young law students and the girls who attended Mrs. Sarah Pierce's Female Seminary, Litchfield was a lively place in 1822. Mrs. Pierce's rules were strict: rise early, dress neatly, exercise before breakfast, attend church every Sunday unless for such a good reason that it could be presented "at the Day of Judgment," study closely for at least two hours outside the classroom, and attend no public ball or sleighing party until 16 years of age. At the same time, Mrs. Pierce believed that girls should have social graces, and shared their belief that they should also have good times. Parties were given at the Female Seminary to which the law students were invited, and parties were given at the homes where the girls and the law students boarded. There was little trouble in Litchfield between the students and the townspeople, who treated the students as their own sons and daughters. What with sleighing parties and musicales, songfests and dances, suppers and whist parties, life in Litchfield offered much play along with hard work.

At school, Horace excelled, as it was beginning to appear he always did. Several students had been admitted to the bar before coming to the law school, and others had superior educational advantages. Nevertheless, Horace more than held his own with all of them.

Judge Gould lectured from carefully prepared notes, and he expected the students to take down every word. These notes would be the students' law books in the years to come, and some would never have any others. Moot court—a mock court held for purposes of practicing argument on hypothetical cases—was held once a week. Judge Gould always presided. The question of law to be argued was presented a week ahead by the Judge, and two students each were assigned to both sides. Horace Mann was elected by his fellow students to the highest office under the Judge, "attorney-general."

Horace, with his love of debate and oratory, shone at moot court. His arguments were distinguished for their clearness. Once Horace's case was opposed by a decision Judge Gould had previously given. Fellow students were of the opinion that Horace had made out the best case. Judge Gould, too, seemed to share that opinion, for after reading his supporting arguments, he answered some of Horace's points. The students felt that he did so with "some exhibition of improper feeling or wounded self-esteem."

Horace's fellow student, J. W. Scott, left Litchfield with the conviction that Horace Mann would be one of the great names of his time. His one possible drawback, Scott felt, was that he might lack the needed physical vigor. But Horace's health during his Litchfield days was better than it had been for some time. He worked hard, he needed money, but he was happy, and he found the Connecticut climate to his liking.

After more than a year of study at Litchfield, Mann

entered the office of Judge James Richardson of Dedham, Massachusetts, in May of 1823, and worked in his office until the following December, when he was admitted to practice in the Dedham courts. Judge Richardson's influence was largely cultural. The Judge had been the class poet of Harvard in 1797, and was an untiring student of literature as well as of law. These facts impressed Horace, who was inclined to distrust culture even as he tried to embrace it. Judge Richardson's writing, even in legal papers, was "marked by purity, grace and beauty of form." Horace learned something about the use of words.

Dedham itself influenced Horace Mann's growth. When he went there, Dedham was a beautiful, little New England town—beautiful but not quiet. Its citizens had minds of their own, and they had not always liked lawyers. In 1786 they had instructed their representatives in the Legislature to try to introduce such regulations into the courts of law and such restraints on the order of lawyers that the Dedham citizens might find "our security, and not our ruin, in them. If, upon a fair discussion and mature deliberation, such a measure should appear impracticable, you are to endeavor that the order of lawyers be totally abolished."

Yet, when Mann entered the practice of law in Dedham in 1823, several other lawyers were engaged in successful practices there, and Welcome Burgess wrote him that "perhaps there is no place in New England better calculated for a young lawyer than Dedham, provided he intends ultimately to remove to the 'literary emporium.'" (The "literary emporium," of course, was Boston.)

Perhaps just because the Dedham citizens had minds of their own and the lovely village was so constantly filled with controversy, it was calculated to be a good place for a young lawyer.

One of the most interesting and typical controversies of Dedham involved the Dedham Parish of the First Church. The Parish entered into a lawsuit in 1823 because a number of the parishioners wanted a Unitarian minister and also wanted to retain the First Church property, and a number of other parishioners wanted no part of a Unitarian minister but also wanted to retain the church property. The case was decided in favor of the people who wanted the right to have a Unitarian minister, and the Congregationalists in the church removed themselves to a church across the street. All over New England, the fight between the liberal Unitarians and the orthodox Congregationalists or "Trinitarians" went on. In Dedham, Horace Mann joined the Unitarians.

Clients, at first were slow to come to Mann, but he took advantage of this early slack period to study exhaustively the principles of law. He said afterward that his mastery of these at this time had given him an "unfailing capital" on which to draw in time of need.

He made it a cardinal rule never to take a case in which he did not believe. Some years later in writing to a young lawyer who had asked for his advice, he said, "Never espouse the wrong side of a cause knowingly; and if unwittingly you find yourself on the wrong side, leap out of it as quickly as you would jump out of a vat of boiling brimstone. . . . It is utterly amazing to me how a man can trifle with his own mind. I do not mean, now, his mind considered as a part of his immortal self, but his mind considered as the mere instrument with which he works. . . .

[*36*]

What would you think of a poor barber who should batter the edge of his razors against flint, as preparatory to shaving? Well, that would be wisdom . . . compared with the man who would wear off the edge of his conscience against known error . . . I well know, for I have often heard, what the old lawyers say about its being right to defend a known wrong side. I deny it all and despise it. If a bad man wants such work done, he shall not have my soul to do it with. . . ."

But though Mann had few cases at the beginning of his practice, he had stature from the first in the eyes of the Dedham townspeople. They chose him to be the Fourth of July speaker in 1823, a signal honor, since Fourth of July orations throughout New England were the most important speeches of the year. He wrote to Lydia, "I am expected to put a black gown on . . . and shall have a right to make a noise for half an hour for my own amusement, other folks in the meantime being bound to hold their tongues." In his address he suggested, as he had done before and would do many times over during his lifetime, "That intelligence is to a republican government what life is to the animal system."

Horace Mann was popular in Dedham, partly perhaps because he was a young lawyer with a warm smile and agreeable wit and manners and an eligible young bachelor, but mainly because of his intelligence and worth. He had a wide circle of friends, of many ages and interests. He belonged to an organized reading club that had its own library. He went on boating and walking excursions with friends, among whom were Catherine and Elizabeth Haven, daughters of Judge Haven. The large and beautiful Haven home was frequently the center of social activities. Cathe-

rine, writing later about Horace at this period, said that he
was brilliant in general conversation. "His droll sayings
could never be recalled without exciting a hearty laugh at
their originality. . . . His originality was so refreshing, so
exciting, because he treated the most trifling subjects in
a manner peculiar to himself." He had a power of drawing
out other minds: "The timid ones, who usually hardly dared
express themselves on grave and weighty topics, would rise
from a *tête-à-tête* with him, wondering at the amount of
talent, thought, and feeling he had opened, and the chord
of sympathy he had touched."

But even Catherine, for all her admiration, recognized
that Mann's "was too strong a nature not to come sometimes
in collision with the opinions and prejudices, perhaps with
the principles, of other individuals, by whom, consequently,
his true character could not be appreciated."

He came into conflict with some of these individuals on
the subject of temperance. A temperance club was formed by
some of Dedham's citizens not long after Mann's arrival, and
he joined it, and became its president.

Horace had been brought up in a time and place where
ardent spirits were commonly used. He often said that he
and all his playmates were educated to become drunkards:
"Many of them became so; and such was the imminence of
my own peril, that when I look back to my early life, I feel
like a soldier coming out of battle who puts his hand up to
his head to see if it is on." As a student he found that
spirits dulled him mentally, and decided that he had no
right to impair his health. Yet, he drank wine occasionally
for some years, and at the time he accepted the presidency
of the Dedham temperance club, he did not seek to bring

about the total abolition of drinking, but rather to bring about temperateness. He thought that education about the effects of alcoholic spirits could bring about moderation in their use.

In those days political candidates "treated" the voters with liquor in order to curry favor. Later, when Mann ran for the General Court, or Massachusetts legislature, in 1827, he broke the custom. Thinking, however, that his move might be mistaken for miserliness, he gave to charity more than he would have spent on such a treat. He was elected.

Advocacy of the temperance cause at this time in Massachusetts, as elsewhere in the country, frequently brought with it reproach, disdain, and a loss of professional business. Although Mann was later to become a drinker of water only, he was no fanatic. In 1837, when he became Secretary of the Massachusetts Board of Education, he was a member of both the Council of the Massachusetts State Temperance Society and president of the Suffolk County Temperance Society. Both these offices he resigned so as not to have to fight two battles at the same time. Although both were in the cause of education, as he saw it the battle for the public schools quite outweighed in importance the one for temperance.

But this was still in the future. Horace Mann's espousal of the temperance movement has been frequently misunderstood because he continued to have wine, and even brandy at times, for years to come. It should be remembered that he began by seeking, through education, to bring about moderateness in drinking rather than total abolition.

Mann's affairs went increasingly well. Cases began to come to him, and court records show that in his 14 years of legal practice, "he gained at least four out of five of all the contested cases in which he was engaged." His inflexible rule of never taking a case unless he believed it to be right gave him, with this conscious conviction that he was contending for the truth, a magnetism that he would not otherwise have had. He said that he only wanted the opportunity to be put in communication with a jury to "impregnate them with my own belief."

His trial methods suggest methods that can be used in many situations. He always summarized every part of his argument with a vivid statement that the jury could remember when they retired to deliberate. He used telling examples and figures of speech, too, for the same purpose. He tried to give each juror something he could "quote" to his fellow jurors. He argued cases as if he too were in the jury room, considering pro's and con's. Juries were confident of his honesty, and they remembered his illustrations.

Mann was elected Town Moderator of Dedham in 1824, and was reelected in 1827, 1828, 1830, and 1831. The Town Moderator's was an important office. At that time, New England towns were small enough so they could be governed by their own town meetings, over which the moderator presided. At appointed times, all voters gathered to argue and then to vote directly on any problems having to do with the running of the town's affairs. Many New England towns, including Dedham, still hold such town meetings. This method of government is the heart of the democratic process, for every voter thus has a direct say in how things are run, how money is spent, what plans are made for the future. The moderator's influence is felt not only through his chairmanship of meetings, but also in his appointment of the committees to carry out the policies determined in the meetings. In such a turbulent town as Dedham was in Horace Mann's time, the moderator had to be open-minded but firm, he had to know his law, and he had to know the town voters and their needs.

Horace Mann was asked to be a public orator for Dedham again in 1826. On that Fourth of July, Thomas Jefferson, the third President, died at his home in Monticello, Virginia, and John Adams, the second President, died at his home in Quincy, Massachusetts. The nation mourned two of its great men. Memorial orations were made for them everywhere. The people of Dedham mourned for John Adams, not only as a great man but as a man who was one of their own—a New Englander, who had known their thoughts and needs and ways—a friend and a neighbor. On July 31, 1826, all of Dedham gathered to hear Mann's address in memory of John Adams and Thomas Jefferson.

John Quincy Adams, then President of the United States, was there, as were his brother, his two sons, and members of his administration.

History has passed down the picture of John Quincy Adams as being extremely capable with a long history of government service, but cold and unbending by nature, with few friends, popular with neither Congress nor the mass of people. A committee of Dedham citizens had prepared a list for him of the people they thought might be sufficiently important to warrant meeting him. The committee asked him to check the ones he would like most to meet. He would have none of it, saying that he wanted to meet everyone interested in meeting him.

Following Horace's oration, John Quincy Adams noted

in his diary that Mann's eulogy of his father and Thomas Jefferson was "of splendid composition and lofty eloquence."

Among other things, Mann had said, "I know not how it may be with those who were contemporary with the mighty deeds of these mighty men—who marked their gradual rise and successive achievements; but for myself I find it difficult to think of them under the mere form and features of individuals. The mention of their names does not so much excite the image of a person as of a long and splendid series of magnificent events. When they are spoken of, the

Orations were orations in those days.

idea is not of shape and statute, but of a people redeemed and a nation born,—of tyrants blenching and sinking from their thrones—of institutions that for so many centuries had bound in and crushed the godlike energies of the human soul, annihilated; and of other institutions adapted to bring the noble image back to some resemblance of its Divine original, spreading from clime to clime and from nation to nation, till the whole globe shall rejoice in the riches of their beneficence." Orations were orations in those days, and his audience would have been disappointed if Mann had spoken in less grandiloquent terms.

Horace Mann had other honors from his fellow citizens. Besides being elected Town Moderator, he was elected to the Dedham School Committee in 1828, and was to be elected again and again in the years following. More importantly to his political career, he was elected in 1827 to be representative for the town of Dedham in the Massachusetts Legislature.

Though one of the youngest members of the House, and in his first term, Mann was not one to be seen and not heard when topics came up that were near to his heart. Also, knowing his home community, he knew that the citizens expected security, not ruin, from their lawyers, and wanted to be represented by someone who would truly represent them through discussion and debate on the important topics that would come before the legislature.

Early in the session, such a topic came up. For years in Massachusetts, all religious opinions had been equal before the law. Now a proposal was made to create estates in a kind of mortmain (literally, "dead hand") control in support and for the benefit of a particular creed or set of doctrines forever afterward. Mann saw the proposal as a threat to religious liberty. He said that to recognize the mortmain law was to transfer one of the worst of medieval institutions into the modern period. His conviction that his belief was both morally and legally correct carried him to his feet against the bill in the face of overwhelming numbers for it.

Mann's opposition to the bill was unexpected. In an earnest and impassioned manner, he laid down the great principles of religious freedom and equality, and exposed the injustice of the proposal, which he felt was the very essence of bigotry, designed to petrify religious opinions. The lecture on religious history he gave the assemblage had a profound effect. Not only did his speech cause the rejection of the bill, but it produced such an effect that no similar attempt has been made since at any time in Massachusetts.

Mann's second speech was in behalf of railroads. This speech, the first printed in the United States favoring the encouragement of railroads, was made at a time when railroads were generally regarded with the contempt later displayed towards the "horseless carriages." The railroads were considered not only dangerous but against God's rules. Opponents said that if He had intended man to be carried so swiftly, He would have given human beings the speed with which to do it.

Mann's speech was modern in its conception, and logical in its presentation. He pointed out that the soil of Massachusetts "scarcely produces anything spontaneously, and scantily requites the most devoted labors of the husbandman." He had had experience with the effort needed to produce anything on Massachusetts soil, and he undoubtedly spoke from his heart. He told of the need Massachusetts had for finding faster ways to bring in grain from neighboring states. He believed that "Machinery is an enlargement of human power. . . . an addition to the organs with which nature has supplied us. . . . and that operations too nice and delicate for the human hand are performed by machinery with an exactness and precision" that the human being could not achieve. He believed always that railroads "would advance to a degree almost beyond our ability to comprehend the interests of agriculture, of common manufacturing and the mechanic arts," and that they were "essential to the continued prosperity of all those branches of business."

On the basis of Mann's first speech in behalf of railroads, the House authorized a railroad survey to cost not more than $10,000.

These were busy days for Horace Mann, and he must have loved every one of them.

His qualities of leadership were recognized, he took an active part in discussions, and he became a conspicuous and leading member of the House. He was early appointed on a committee to report rules for the House. He became chairman of the Judiciary Committee. He reported a bill for lessening "in certain cases, the penalty of arson, burglary and larceny." The penalty at that time was usually the death sentence.

He reported a bill for the regulation and restriction of the rights of public houses to sell liquor.

He protested the practice of rushing measures through the House without due consideration, and censured those members who neglected to examine the measures on which they voted.

He took a leading part in putting through laws that

greatly restricted the traffic in lottery tickets.

Anything having to do with education and religious freedom found in him a champion. His voice was raised always in behalf of the poor, the ignorant, and the unfortunate, regardless of the powerful people who might be opposed.

The people of Dedham had reason to have confidence in their distinguished fellow citizen and representative.

Chapter 4

Change

Change was in the air throughout the country. It was overdue. People in the United States thought on the brave words of 50 years before in the Declaration of Independence, "Life, Liberty, and the pursuit of Happiness." They saw that their country was young and vital and rich in resources; there was enough for all. They saw at the same time misery and injustice, poverty and ignorance on all sides. A number of people set about doing something to make things right.

First in the popular mind was slavery. Massachusetts was a hotbed of the strongest reforming element, the Abolitionists. These men called for the instant and total destruction of the institution of slavery. William Lloyd Garrison at their head published the Abolitionist newspaper, *The Liberator,* in Boston. Though Mann and his friends all opposed slavery, none were in the van of the organized fight. Edward Loring, the Boston attorney and Mann's old friend from the Litchfield school, with his elegant manners matching his noble ideas was said to have made antislavery fashionable in Boston. Mann's attitude toward antislavery, an attitude that many people misunderstood, was fairly complicated. He

[47]

was fighting for education for everyone. He once said that he would give his life to what men called "freeing the slaves," but not his faith. "What the anti-slavery movement wants to do I say inescapably must be done, but surely I can take no great faith in a world in which the Negroes have merely been brought up to our poor level?"

Some people—not many but some influential ones— turned their scrutiny upon the prison system and the treatment of the insane. Reform there was long overdue. In the early 19th century, people could be imprisoned for the most trivial crimes, and forced to spend years—sometimes their lifetimes—in jails and prisons, cruelly treated and without benefit of legal counsel. Insane people, too, were frequently committed to prison for want of any other place to put them. Insanity was looked upon as a disgrace rather than a sickness, and the insane were often treated as criminals. The insane could be sent to prison, possibly to spend years, chained in cells without heat and light, forgotten by all.

For more than two years a report had been before the Massachusetts Legislature telling of the treatment of the insane in jails and workhouses. The report came into Horace Mann's hands, and he read it carefully. He talked it over with prominent members of the Legislature and some philanthropic citizens of Dedham and Boston. He hoped to establish a climate of opinion in which improvements could be made.

It did not take Mann long to see that the preliminary report and his own persuasions would never bring about action. Typically, he set about securing facts and more facts for the Legislature. With him, always, facts were weapons to be used for the betterment of mankind. The facts he turned up about the "lunatics" of Massachusetts were sufficiently appalling to command attention. His survey of 114 towns, covering half the population of Massachusetts, disclosed 298 insane persons. A few of these were in private homes, and a few others in private sanitariums. But the majority were confined in poorhouses, houses of correction, or jails.

One insane man had been in prison for 28 years. Although usually calm, he was driven into frenzies when the guards brought crowds of people to view him as a public exhibit. He was not allowed to have a fire, and many nights he had not lain down for fear of freezing. He had not been shaved for 28 years.

An old insane man of 70 had been chained for 25 years, and his chain had been taken off only once during that time.

The insane were more often than not confined in unheated, dark inner cells, were frequently chained, were unbathed, unshaved, and with only the most minimum of their human needs attended to. People paid guards money to look at the insane, regarding their ravings as comic antics to be laughed and jeered at. The zoos where wild animals are kept today would have been considered centers of luxury and enlightenment by the insane of that day.

Mann visited the Hartford Retreat for the Insane in Connecticut, a private sanitarium. This institution had been opened in 1824, with Dr. Eli Todd, a medical graduate of Yale, in charge. Todd's beliefs were revolutionary in that day. He believed that if the patient was in good physical condition, his mental functions were still operative. He be-

[49]

lieved that many people who suffered the most sudden and violent outbursts of insanity were the most easily restored, and he cited many instances in support of this belief. He had the modern theory that insanity was a sickness of the mind, and that the insane person was no more to be blamed than someone who was physically ill. Dr. Todd found in Mann an eager pupil for his teachings. Mann came away from his visit to the Retreat with the vision of a home for all the insane of Massachusetts, supported by public funds, with Dr. Todd at its head.

In 1830, Horace Mann's efforts on behalf of the insane of Massachusetts were rewarded. On March 8, $30,000 was appropriated by the Legislature for the erection of a "Lunatic Hospital." Mann's speech for the appropriation was reported at length in the leading newspaper of the state with the comment, "We have not heard a speech during the session which seemed to occupy more of the individual attention of the House than Mr. Mann's."

Not all of Mann's acts and thoughts during 1829 and 1830 were directed solely to the public good.

On June 9, 1829, he addressed a formal proposal of marriage to Charlotte Messer, youngest daughter of Dr. Asa Messer, who had been President of Brown University when Mann was an undergraduate and later a tutor there.

For 13 years now, Horace Mann had been a visitor in the Messer home, a respected and well regarded guest. During all this time he had known Charlotte, whose loveliness and kindness and gaiety had stayed in his heart from the days of her childhood. He waited until he had reached a position of some success in his profession and in public life, until he had paid the debts for his education, and until he had some money in the bank—and probably, also, until Charlotte had reached a suitable age for marriage—before proposing to her.

The proposal was a written one. Charlotte delayed in replying to it. She was frail. She was the youngest of three children, all girls, and the delight not only of her parents and sisters but of their large circle of friends. Not only because of her frailty, but also because she was lovely, generous, and never unkind or envious or unsympathetic, she was greatly loved and protected. She had grown up in the heart of an untroubled family circle, and in some ways she desired nothing more. She felt that Horace Mann idealized her too much; she said she wished he would see her as she really was. But Horace pursued his suit of this young woman he loved with the intensity he had earlier showed in pursuing an education, and she finally promised to marry him.

In spite of the difference in their ages, Horace's friends and family rejoiced in the betrothal, and the Messer family and friends agreed that it was a good one. Early in 1830 Horace had gone home to Franklin to inform his mother of the engagement. He wrote Charlotte that his mother loved her "by anticipation."

Of the many congratulations from his friends, probably none were more heartfelt than those of Edward Loring, "glorious Neddy," who wrote in an outburst of enthusiasm, "Hallelujah, Cherubim and Seraphim and all glad things and gladdest of them all is no gladder than I— my dear friend."

Charlotte was good for Horace. She had a gaiety and vitality of spirit that not even her frail health could keep

[*51*]

down. She teased him as no one else had ever done. He wrote to complain about the brevity of her letters. "It cannot but occur to you that a just notion of economy forbids any part of a sheet unoccupied." Charlotte replied that the blank space on a page would rest his eyes. Horace complained about the granite-hearted postmaster who did not have a letter from Charlotte to give to him. Charlotte suggested that he should petition the President to have the postmaster removed.

Horace worried constantly about Charlotte's health. He wrote her that he could not bear to see her look so interestingly pale. A saint, he said, did not look less saintly to him just because she was blooming with health.

Charlotte did not always tease. Once she wrote in answer to a letter in which Horace spoke almost despairingly about another postponement in their marriage, "I have acknowledged to you that I loved you, I have given you what I consider *very* strong proof of love in consenting to leave family and friends so dear to me as mine are, to share with you the happiness, or misery of life. . . . I never doubted the sincerity of your love—do me the justice, I beg you, to place equal confidence in my sincerity. Without mutual confidence we can never be happy, we should be without an anchor."

The marriage of Charlotte Messer and Horace Mann took place in Providence, Rhode Island, on September 29, 1830. Charlotte was 21. Horace was 34.

They moved to Dedham, where they had a home at the corner of Church Street and Franklin Square. It was a fair and substantial home, furnished carefully and lovingly by Horace and Charlotte. It quickly became the center

[52]

of the social and intellectual life of the town. Charlotte visited her neighbors, and they visited her. At one home, she told Horace she had met and been greatly attracted to a young woman, Miss Sophia Peabody of Salem. Neither she nor Horace could have had any clairvoyant feeling what that Miss Peabody would one day mean to Horace Mann.

Charlotte and Horace Mann knew happiness. Many people remember afterward that they were happy at a particular period of their lives, while at the time they complained of their lot and did not know of their happiness. This was not the case with Horace Mann. Charlotte was his first love, they cared deeply for one another, and he knew that he had a happiness that is rare upon this earth. About this period of his life Mann wrote that there was, for him, "a light upon earth brighter than any light of the sun, a voice sweeter than any of nature's harmonies." He did not think "but that the happiness, which was boundless in present enjoyment, would be perpetual in duration." During this period of his life, he was described by his friends as "radiant."

These days were busy ones for Horace Mann, and days of happiness and fulfillment. While engrossed in some piece of business, he had only to let his mind steal away for a minute to "her lovely image" to feel refreshed. He loved success, he knew, and now doubly so because it added to Charlotte's enjoyment. He had valued distinction for its own sake, but now he valued it doubly because of the pleasure he thought it gave Charlotte.

Since 1827 Mann had been Dedham's representative in the House of the Massachusetts legislature. It was increasingly recognized that his combination of ability, integrity, and organizational skills made him invaluable. He was an associate one could depend upon. He was an opponent to be reckoned with. The recognition of his quality brought with it increased duties and demands.

Having got the bill passed for the erection of an insane asylum, Mann was not to be allowed to stop his efforts on behalf of the undertaking. Undoubtedly he would have been disappointed if it had been otherwise. On June 25, 1830, Governor Levi Lincoln had appointed Mann, as one of three commissioners to carry through the establishing and building of the "Lunatic Hospital". It was to be located in Worcester. By September of 1830, the commissioners could report that the north wing of the asylum was ready for the roof, and the center and south wings were more than half completed. There was some disagreement about a dome for the building. One commissioner thought the building would look heavy without one, and $500 or $600 would cover the costs. Some legislators felt that a gilded dome would be good advertising for the asylum. Mann held firmly against this. Public funds were not to be used for anything as unessential as a gilded dome, he said. No dome was added.

By 1831 the demands upon Mann's time were enormous. He was occupied with his own law practice and was an attorney to the Supreme Judicial Court. He supervised the building of the asylum and met with his fellow commissioners to make decisions about the present and plans for the future. He was on a number of important committees in the Legislature and was instrumental in introducing and supporting a number of important bills.

During that year a Congressional Temperance Party was formed, and Mann became president of the Suffolk County Temperance Society. He was the most prominent member of a committee of the Legislature to change the license law so that county commissioners could grant licenses to public houses without the right of selling ardent spirits. He wanted to see an end to the "grog shops" throughout Massachusetts where men could buy raw whiskey cheaply and thus become objects of despair and recklessness. He said: "There are thousands and tens of thousands of inebriates who never would have been so had the tavern and the dramshop been five miles off from their homes." The grog shops were a special menace to the thousands of immigrants pouring into New England from Ireland and other countries. Without money, frequently without work, homesick, resented and discriminated against by the native American people, these people sought to find the fulfillment of their dreams of a free and prosperous country in the one place they were sure of a welcome—the grog shop. Opponents to Mann pointed out bitterly that the stand he took was against the poor of the land, not the rich. The fact that he fought most of his fights for the poor was never pointed out to the immigrants, who could not read his speeches and never heard them.

Mann's speech on the licensing of public houses was a "shower of eloquence" according to one of his opponents, who did not intend his words as a compliment. In spite of opposition, the bill for regulation passed, 155 to 69. The opposition was stronger than the vote would indicate. Many men were opposed to the bill privately who would not have been returned to the Legislature by their districts if they had been opposed to it publicly.

Edward Loring wrote Mann that Silas Holbrook, a close friend of both of them, "says you are the coming representative. . . . I am glad of it, but you will have a stormy time. Much is expected of you. The few honest, wise, moral people depend upon a steady, unflinching and able defense of the principles of the License Law, against a ferocious and reckless opposition, and you are before the House and the public as the champion of sobriety and morality and public virtue, and godfather of the statute. . . . The best men in society depend on your inclination and ability, and desire to trust their cause to you; so Atlas must spread his shoulders."

In 1831, Mann worked hard to get changes made in the law "allowing imprisonment for debt," and to liberalize the laws concerning the attachment of property. To do so was unthinkable to some people.

"If a man can't be jailed for not paying debts," his opponents cried, "then no bills will be paid, and we'll all be ruined!"

"If a man's property can't be taken in payment of debts," they cried, "then bills will be forever unpaid."

Mann's sense of logic quite as much as his humanitarianism was outraged. Some of his most cutting words were delivered on the subject of distinguishing the fraudulent debtor from the debtor who could not pay because of illness or misfortune. How can a man earn the money with which to pay his debt, Mann asked, if he is languishing in prison or has had the tools of his trade confiscated? Again, Mann was far ahead of his time. Imprisonment for debt was not abolished in any country until England passed the Debtors' Act in 1869. It was many years before England's example was followed in the United States.

In 1831, also, Mann worked to abolish capital punishment "of persons convicted of stealing, in certain cases." He also moved to instruct the Committee on the Judiciary to provide that capital punishment should be inflicted in as private a manner as possible. Public hangings, even in that "literary emporium," Boston, were regarded as excellent and acceptable public entertainment.

One appointment Horace Mann received in 1831—one that proved a major nuisance later although it helped his political career, was his commission by Governor Lincoln as Judge-Advocate of the First Division of Militia of the Commonwealth. He was now Major Mann.

In one way or another Mann was taken away from home much more than he liked, and Charlotte spent long weeks with her family in Providence to help fight both loneliness and poor health. Once Horace had thought they might move to Boston, where they could enjoy the variety of city living and could be together more. But Charlotte had told him before their marriage that she was but a "simple country damsel," and she held to this, however much her tongue must have been in her cheek when she first said it.

There was a dark shadow always with Horace these days. Charlotte always felt that her health was getting better. Horace had been convinced that under his care she would gain a health she had never known. Charlotte's health, however, did not get better. Unlike fictionalized love stories, where two people can love each other greatly and be able to seclude themselves from the world around them, Horace and Charlotte Mann were living out their lives as it appeared they must. The very love that made Horace want to accomplish all things good for Charlotte's sake frequently took him from her. The very love that she had for him, and her own natural hopefulness, made her pretend to him that she had considerably better health than she had.

At this point of seriousness and commitment in both Mann's private and public life, a comic opera episode occurred. From March 5th to March 29th and again from April 10th to April 14th in 1832, Major Mann was called up for his first—and his only—duty as Judge-Advocate of the First Division of Militia of the Commonwealth. In this capacity, he had to help conduct the trial by court martial of Lieutenant Colonel Granville Temple Winthrop on charges preferred against him by the orders of Governor Lincoln. The whole story is a farcical one, one in which the Governor himself seems to have been the principal culprit.

On January 4, 1832, the Massachusetts legislature reconvened under a new ruling that abolished the short spring session. The Independent Corps of Cadets, a company of the First Division composed mostly of college students and clerks, was commanded by young Lieutenant Colonel Winthrop. Governor Lincoln ordered the Corps to escort the Governor, state officials, and members of the Legislature to Old South Meeting House for the Election Sermon, and afterward to escort them back to the State House. This was the first public occasion on which Winthrop had commanded the cadets, and the first time the Election Sermon had been given in January rather than in May.

Following custom, the cadets were not invited into the church to hear the sermon, but were ordered to be dismissed and to be back in half an hour.

January 4th was one of the coldest days of that winter in Boston; it was five degrees and there were three feet of snow. The cadets were not accustomed to extreme cold. They were not adequately dressed, and many of them were without overshoes. They were no doubt delighted to be dismissed for a half-hour, which they spent in the warmth of the Exchange Coffee House. When they returned to the church, the sermon was still going on. After waiting around for 15 or 20 minutes, Winthrop decided that in view of the extreme temperature, they should return to the Coffee House. They came back to the church again in about 15 minutes; the sermon still continued. Again, Winthrop marched the cadets off to the Coffee House. Upon the summons of a messenger, they returned a third time to the church. This time, they found that the service had finally ended, and that Governor Lincoln was some blocks away, returning to the State House. Winthrop hurried after him and apologized, but the Governor rejected the apology.

Winthrop pleaded not guilty at the court martial. He contended that such escort duty was not legal, since martial law could be invoked only in time of national emergency, and this escort had been an act of courtesy only. The Governor contended that the honor of the State had been sullied, which seemed somewhat odd since two previous governors had been faced with similar mishaps, and had accepted the apologies of the colonels, and had let it go at that.

Horace Mann's legal position was that Winthrop's contention was not well founded. He said that martial law was not involved one way or another, but only an act of military offense, over which the court martial did have jurisdiction. He said that having accepted the order from the Governor voluntarily and without protest at the time, Winthrop was under obligation to perform his task. With this opinion, the court agreed.

As the trial droned on, everyone connected with it—

with the possible exception of the Governor—got bored. It was difficult to know why the Governor should demand so much time from a number of busy people, and carry so much rancor over a simple mishap that he could have prevented by remaining at the church for a few minutes until his escort returned, or that he could have met gracefully by accepting the apology. Some thought that his whole position resulted from his being at odds with his Lieutenant Governor, the father of young Lieutenant Colonel Winthrop.

Horace Mann's attitude as the trial extended beyond the meetings of the Legislature can be judged from one of his notes to Charlotte: "Day after day I resort to the temple where the sons of Mars are assembled to vindicate the tarnished honor of his Godship." He was sick to death of the trial, and wanted to get home to Dedham.

This once, apparently, Mann, as Judge-Advocate of the First Division, was forced into defending a position in which he did not much believe. He handled himself well personally and as a lawyer, however, and earned a reputation that was greatly responsible for getting him elected to the State Senate less than three years later.

The case could only be called a moral victory for the Governor. Young Winthrop was found not guilty of eight of the nine counts against him, and was sentenced to be reprimanded in orders—a reprimand which Governor Lincoln took 6,000 words to deliver. Winthrop was also ordered discharged from arrest and restored to his command. Finally, he had a book published at his own expense to give *his* version of what happened.

Thus began and ended the military career of Major Mann, and Horace Mann went home to Dedham.

Horace carried Charlotte tenderly into the garden.

The shining hours Horace and Charlotte Mann spent together were almost over. Charlotte's health, never good, became worse in the spring and summer of 1832. Mann cancelled meeting after meeting to be with her. Mary Messer, Charlotte's sister, came from Providence to help take care of her. In July, Horace wrote his sister, Lydia: . . . she bears her illness with the stoicism of a philosopher and the resignation of a saint. . . ."

Horace carried his young wife from her bed to a favorite chair or into the garden. He read aloud to her. He sat in the dusk and held her hand. He and Mary prepared delicate and special foods to tempt her appetite. She seemed better, and Mary returned to Providence.

At last, though, on the night of July 31, 1832, Charlotte Mann's life came to a close. Horace was alone beside her.

From 11 until 2 o'clock, her struggle with death went on. She died in the early morning hours of August 1, in delirium, not recognizing Horace. She was 23 years of age, and they had been married less than two years. The cause of her death has never been fully explained. She had never been strong. She probably had tuberculosis.

Horace Mann never wholly recovered from the agonizing effects of that night's vigil.

He did the things that had to be done, hardly knowing what he was doing. He took Charlotte's body to Providence, where it was buried in the old North Burial Ground. On her tombstone are inscribed the words, "This mortal shall put on immortality."

With a terrible desire to put from him the agony of remembrance, he sold their household furnishings except for a few pieces he sent to the Messer family. He resigned all his offices, including his seat in the legislature.

Dr. Messer wrote tenderly to his "dear son": "Mr. Gay has just brought us the trunks and chair of our dear Charlotte. They, though we are exceedingly glad to receive them, have covered us with a flood of tears. . . . By saying [earlier] that I hoped all the furniture might go to your personal comfort, I meant that whatever part of it you might retain for your own use might still, by being changed into something else, subserve that very comfort; and that we might, as far as we can recollect it, carry into effect the *will* of our dear daughter; fully assured that her will would, in the highest degree, secure your personal comfort. . . . I say solemnly that. . . . I have as implicit, unconditional, absolute confidence in you as I have or can have in any person on earth. . . ."

[*62*]

Dr. Messer added a postscript: "I pray you, my dear Horace, take care of your health. Go about, and give yourself abundant exercise. Last year, perhaps this year, Judge Story buried an interesting daughter. The affliction was overwhelming. Some time after, a friend asked the Judge why he worked so hard. He answered, 'I must, or die.' May God Almighty bless you!"

With the proceeds from the sale of the furnishings, Mann bought a law library. Charlotte would have liked that, for she had long wanted him to have one. He was to sell it later to advance one of his causes, as he had earlier sold his set of Homer to get to Litchfield; but for the present it represented a memorial to Charlotte and of their life together.

Horace Mann's friends worried not only for his health, but for his sanity. His early and long-tried friend, Silas Holbrook, attended him constantly. Edward Loring beseeched him to take to his broken heart "the consolation that Charlotte has left you and realize, my dear friend, the state of mind she would wish you to be in—the feelings and thoughts that she would wish you to . . . encourage, and then for her sake . . . be steady minded and sustained. Good bye, Horace. My heart aches now and I can't write. God bless and keep you."

Charlotte's brother-in-law, Sydney Williams, urged Mann to join him as a law partner in Taunton.

Against this, Edward Loring urged a partnership with him in Boston: "Your furtherances being greater in a city like Boston, your resources will be best accumulated there, and ten years will find you here richer, intellectually and morally; exerting a wider influence and laying up every day more deeds and thoughts and feelings to pillow your age upon, than a life in Taunton can give you; and it will find you richer in purse, too. A few years will see you at the extent of all things in Taunton, as you now are in Dedham, and what then will your resources be—to rust?" Loring added that he would be an abler, better, and happier lawyer and man if Horace Mann would join him.

In an effort to escape the pain of memories, Mann decided to give up his house and life in Dedham, and to join Loring in Boston. His removal from Dedham did not lessen his grief; and in the months that followed, misfortune seemed to be a constant companion.

First came the death of Silas Holbrook, which caused Mann to write to a friend, "A denser shade of gloom has come over the earth, and my faint heart bleeds anew. There is no man living who loved me so well as my friend Holbrook. I have a thousand times comforted myself with the thought, that if, amid the tempests of life, my character was lost overboard, there was one man who would plunge in to save it. As a friend, it is not enough to say of him, he was true; *he was truth*."

Then came the death of Dr. Messer. Mann observed with sorrow that never had a more firmly linked circle been broken. He felt such sympathy for Mrs. Messer and Charlotte's sisters that he wrote a friend that he "looked upon the dead with envy, and pitied the living because they still lived. I administered consolations [to them] which I did not feel. I can speak to the heart-broken in language they can understand: I am versed in every dialect of sorrow!"

There can be no doubt about Mann's capacity for grief. For many years, on every anniversary of Charlotte's death, Mann shut himself in his room and lived again the wild and lonely vigil of the throes of his final night with her.

On the fifth anniversary of Charlotte's death, he wrote that "this fated night has come, and again is visibly present before me that scene of anxiety, of dismay, of struggle and of death, and of the agony of the surviving, worse than a thousand deaths, through which, five years ago tonight, I passed. . . . Oh! what months of gloom and solitude I have passed through."

But a quieter note had now come in. Mann concluded, five years after Charlotte's death, that these hours of suffering must end: "To that end, distant or near—still distant, however near—I must look. Every anniversary brings me nearer to it."

Chapter 5

Boston Boardinghouse

W hen Horace Mann decided to join Edward Loring as a partner in 1833, he took the advice of a friend, and rented a room at Mrs. Clarke's boardinghouse, behind the State House. There were many such boardinghouses in Boston, owned and managed by women of good family, sometimes because they needed the money, sometimes because they wanted the companionship their boarders provided. Mrs. Clarke was the daughter of a minister and the mother of a minister to be, James Freeman Clarke, who was soon to graduate from Harvard Theological Seminary. She needed the money. She was also a talkative woman, and the table in her dining room, where all her boarders ate together, was a news center for her. There she could both give and receive the latest gossip of the day. She needed that, too.

There is nothing today quite comparable to the boardinghouses that studded the United States in the 19th century. There was even then nothing in the United States quite comparable to the ones that studded Boston. Each one had a quality of its own. Each one represented a Boston in miniature.

Elizabeth had Horace's attention, but Mary had his smiles.

[67]

Boston at that time had a population of about 62,000; it was the literary center of the United States with most of America's chief essayists, historians, poets, philosophers, and novelists living in and around the city. It was small enough so that nearly every one knew every one else with similar interests. And it was even then a state of mind as well as a city.

The people gathered around Mrs. Clarke's dining table when Horace Mann moved in were important in themselves. They were also important for the parts they were to play in Mann's life.

Miss Elizabeth Peabody was there—29 years of age, already a personage, known far and wide for her championship of good causes, always moving full tilt into battle with all flags flying. She was a disciple of Dr. William Ellery Channing, a Unitarian minister who was Boston's greatest religious figure at the time; and she had written down from memory for Dr. Channing many of his sermons. He was Boston's conscience, and Elizabeth had been his literary assistant, which made her a kind of keeper of the keys for the Boston conscience.

Elizabeth wanted to go directly to the heart of the mystery of Mann's grief. She had a genius for discovering genius, and for introducing geniuses to other geniuses for their mutual benefit. Among her introductions were those of Jones Very, the least known transcendentalist to Emerson, the best known; the novelist Nathaniel Hawthorne to his future wife, her sister, Sophia; Nathaniel Hawthorne to the historian-collector of the port of Boston, George Bancroft, who gave Hawthorne a job in the Boston customhouse; and Horace Mann to Dr. Channing.

At the time Mann met Elizabeth, she was engaged in writing a history of the ancient Greeks. Mann was more impressed because she could outquote him from the classics than because she could also read French and German, which he could not do. She was a voluble woman, interested in everything under the sun. And she had opinions about everything under the sun—even things she knew little about.

"I know all about your work for the insane asylum, Mr. Mann," she said. "And I want to know everything there is to know about it."

Within a fortnight, she had got Mann aside to inquire into the nature of his grief, for she did not intend to let anyone sit brooding at any table where she was without finding out what he was brooding about. Whatever his trouble, she was sure Dr. Channing could take care of it. When she discovered not only the nature of his grief, but also that his grief had made him doubt the natural goodness of God, she was more than ever sure that Dr. Channing was the person he needed.

Mary Peabody, a younger sister of Elizabeth, was also at that boardinghouse table. In her own way she was as determined and intelligent as Elizabeth, but she had humor as well as conviction, and would never be found charging about the streets collecting strangers because she believed they had either genius or need. She was quieter than Elizabeth, but then, as Mary observed, no one but Mrs. Clarke, could outtalk Elizabeth. Mary was not pretty in any accepted sense of prettiness, but she had a trim figure; lovely, dark eyes; and a firm though gentle mouth. She had a look of distinction about her and dressed with some elegance, even though there was little money to be spent on clothes.

In their sitting room at Mrs. Clarke's boardinghouse, Elizabeth and Mary Peabody ran a select school for girls. Their pupils were the daughters of some of Boston's most illustrious citizens, but the school was considered select principally because of the rigor of its curriculum and the progressive methods the Peabodys used in teaching. Elizabeth, of course, was the headmistress of the school, but Mary was an able assistant. Much of the money which they made, which was never great, was sent home to Salem, where there were younger brothers and another sister, Sophia, five years younger than Mary.

Jared Sparks was also at Mrs. Clarke's boardinghouse. So was Mrs. Sparks, but she was not well, and took her meals in her room. Both Sparks and Mann had considerable reputations in their own fields by now, and they met with interest and came together in a friendship that was to last far beyond their stay at the boardinghouse.

Sparks was seven years older than Mann, and his career, in many ways, had paralleled Mann's. Like Mann, he had risen from the ranks of the New England poor. He had supported himself as a carpenter and by teaching in a country school. He had battled his way into Harvard at 22 where he made a brilliant scholastic record, and had then held a position as tutor at Havre de Grace in Maryland. The inn where Sparks had lived at Havre de Grace was on the post road to Washington, and half the notables of the day stopped there on their way to the capital. Sparks had made influential friends among them, and in 1821 had been appointed chaplain of the United States House of Representatives. Always interested in history, he had been fascinated and stimulated by finding himself in the midst of its making. In 1823 he had left the Unitarian ministry, and purchased the *North American Review*. The *North American* had been from its beginning the arbiter of literature in New England. Under Spark's editorship, it became a financial success as well.

The dining room at Mrs. Clarke's was the scene of continual conflict. Mrs. Clarke was determined to tell all the gossip she knew and to draw from the others gossip she wanted to know. Elizabeth was determined to keep the conversation at a high level. Jared Sparks was both irritated by Elizabeth's way of holding forth on all subjects and determined to give her a respect for historical research, which he felt sure she did not have from the way she seemed to be going about writing her history of the Greeks. Anyhow, Jared Sparks thought it was a waste of time to write about the Greeks. What the United States needed now were historians who would and could record the history of the United States.

Sparks could speak with authority. After all, he had already written a three-volume *Life of Gouverneur Morris*. He had spent months up and down the Atlantic seaboard searching out forgotten documents and letters that would otherwise either have rotted or been burned. At present he was working on *The Life and Writings of George Washington,* a work containing thousands of original letters and papers, many of which he himself had discovered in attics and trunks and trash bins all along the eastern seaboard. There would be 12 volumes to Washington's life by the time Sparks finished, and there would be another 10 volumes devoted to Franklin, with many more historical writings to come.

Sparks aroused indignation and vehement protest from Elizabeth; and Horace Mann, in spite of himself, frequently found himself drawn into the battle—first on one side and then on the other—and drawn out of his shell.

George Hillard was there, too. He had known the Peabody family for some years. Just graduated from Harvard Law School and soon to be admitted to the bar, he was living at Mrs. Clarke's principally because Jared Sparks was staying there. Although he was to become the law partner of the great Charles S. Sumner, Hillard was never much interested in the law, but wanted to be a writer. Now he was spending all his spare time and some he could not spare working on a *Life of John Smith* for Spark's "Library of American Biography." He had an idea for editing the English poet, Edmund Spenser's work, and was making elaborate notes and interpretations. He was to become a friend of Hawthorne and of the poet Henry Wadsworth Longfellow and of other famous writers of his day. Although he would earn his living with his legal practice, he always felt most at ease with writers, who were objects of his particular respect and affection.

Never saying much at the table was Samuel Downer, not the last of the boarders at Mrs. Clarke's but the last of the ones who would be important to Horace Mann. Downer was a young man without much formal education. He was just starting out in the business of selling high quality whale oil. He was to make his own and others' fortunes with his oil business. Mann was attracted by Downer's courtesy, modesty, and common sense. The friendship of these two men was to last through differences of political opinions and views about what education should and could be; and until the end of Mann's life, Downer was his trusted friend and business adviser. "Mr. Samuel Downer," Mary Peabody noted, was "always sagacious, independent, true to principle, unambitious, but full of insight into public men and measures, deep in heart, faithful in adversity."

Somewhere along the way, in that boardinghouse in Boston, something happened to Mary Peabody. Elizabeth might get Horace Mann to talk forth his grief. Elizabeth might get his opinions and give him hers on education, government, insane asylums, railroads, and God. Elizabeth might take him to Dr. Channing in order to lead him from religious doubt. Elizabeth might be his confidante and counselor. But one day Horace Mann gave Mary a smile that convinced her that his capacity for happiness was not exhausted, and she "felt the glow permeate every fibre and vein" of her being. Mary, as she confessed many years later, found herself overpowered by the knowledge that the main features of her own ideal of human perfection were not only before her in the person of Horace Mann, but that there was, in him, "something else added." Mary had fallen in love.

So, there they all were, gathered about a boardinghouse table in Boston, a microcosm of Boston.

All of them had the special flavor, the special bent, which these people of changing New England had at the time.

Chapter *6*

Friend of Friendless

T he faces around Mrs. Clarke's boardinghouse table changed. In the summer of 1833, Horace Mann moved to a cot in his law office. The Sparkses moved to Craigie House in Cambridge. In the interest of Sophia's health and at Elizabeth's insistence (and with Elizabeth pulling the strings to make it possible), Mary sailed with Sophia Peabody in December of that year for a sojourn in Cuba that would last until the spring of 1835. Mary admitted later that she went both sadly and gladly. She had come to believe that Horace Mann would never marry again; and she was afraid that if she should remain near him, he would discover her love.

As for Horace Mann, any thoughts of another love or marriage must have been very far away at that time. He moved to his law quarters to live because, through a complicated set of circumstances, he could not afford to stay on at Mrs. Clarke's. He had lent legal and financial assistance to his brother, Stanley, in connection with a couple of manufacturing companies with which Stanley had hoped to make his fortune. Horace himself had become so involved that when Stanley's business failed in 1833, the savings of Horace's professional life were wiped out. Stanley went off to Kentucky to make a new life for himself; but Horace, with his super-refined moral sense, believed it necessary for him to repay Stanley's creditors, and his own, in full. So he moved into his law office. He felt he could withhold nothing from these creditors. For nearly six months he was actually unable to buy dinners half the time. He suffered from hunger, exhaustion, and overwork—and undoubtedly, since he was human— from self pity, as well. But it could not have been otherwise for him. From boyhood, he had been taught to pay his debts as he went, and any debt hanging over him was a millstone holding him down until it could be removed. If he had not been a regular Sunday dinner guest at the Lorings, it is possible he would have broken under the mental and physical strain.

He could not, however, nurse his pride and suffering in dreary solitude forever. There was work to be done; and work, as he had observed at another time and place, was to him what water was to a fish.

The "Lunatic Hospital" at Worcester had just been opened, and Mann's duty to that institution was quite as great as to any creditors. He had to see it through. Governor Lincoln's proclamation to the people of the State of Massachusetts, which was probably written by Mann, had said that, beginning January 10, 1833, there would be a seven weeks' period of admissions, from certain named counties each week. Each county would be allowed to send six of its "lunatics." All arriving inmates were to be clean and clothed. "The Trustees would prefer that the outside dress should be of a mixed color or Oxford gray satinet, and that each patient should come provided with a change of linen,

[75]

and of socks, and a pair of shoes." These clothes must have seemed luxurious to many of the patients, who had never known anything but rags.

Mann had not been successful in persuading Dr. Eli Todd to leave the Hartford Retreat, but he had succeeded in securing Todd's most eminent pupil, Dr. Samuel B. Woodward, as director of the new institution. Woodward, with calm, penetrating, blue eyes and a majestic brow, seemed to have a calming effect on all who came into his presence—including irate legislators.

The hospital had its ups and downs. It was soon insufficient in size for the demands upon it. It was discovered to the sorrow of Mann and Woodward that their belief that no cells would be needed for anyone at any time was unrealistic. Some people, it appeared, did need cells at certain times for their own safety as well as the safety of others.

Nevertheless, only a few years after the opening of the hospital, Mann was able to write to a friend: "When I tell you what has been done for the hospital at Worcester, you will be superstitious, and exclaim, 'It has had an angel.' Dr. Woodward's salary has been raised six hundred dollars. . . . The Legislature has appropriated ten thousand dollars (I write the words out instead of figures, lest you should think I have mistaken the matter of a cipher) to finish the buildings, so that, when done, they will accommodate say two hundred and thirty; seven thousand dollars for the purchase of land, so that our inmates can enjoy the advantages of agricultural employment, which we regard very highly; and three thousand dollars for a chapel, where the oil of religion may be poured in a flood over the ocean of insanity; and eight thousand dollars to meet the current expenses of the institu-

[76]

tion. All this was done without a single audible murmur of opposition; nay, with the greatest apparent cordiality towards the hospital. Besides this, the Senate has empowered its clerk to republish all the reports of the institution in one volume, together with other papers, as he may see fit, with an *ad libitum* authority as to the number of the edition. Enough will be printed to be distributed liberally in every State, and also to be sent to Europe. Ah! I never thought of this when, in 1830, we stormed the dungeons of inhumanity. The outer gates are broken down; and some of the captives are coming forth every day to enjoy the light and the beauty of the physical, and the holier light and beauty of the moral universe: yet here in this midnight silence, as I write, I hear from their more interiour cells, as audibly as if it were the voice of the thunder-cloud, the voices of many victims awaiting in unconsciousness the day of their deliverance."

Any pity that Mann must have felt for himself during the lonely nights in his law office, any suffering that he went through, were both transmitted into a nobler end by reason of the pity he felt for his fellow men and the suffering he went through on their behalf. He would for all his life do whatever he could, however he could, wherever he could to remove the inequalities put upon mankind by ignorance and by handicaps not of the victims' making, such as blindness, insanity, and involuntary servitude.

With the Worcester institution a reality and an inspiration, Miss Dorothea L. Dix—another disciple of Dr. Channing's, who had followed Elizabeth Peabody as a literary assistant to Dr. Channing, much to Elizabeth's disgust—set about reforming the world in behalf of the forgotten insane. She visited 18 state penitentiaries, 300 county jails and houses

[77]

of correction, and over 500 almshouses. Her labors resulted in the establishment of many insane asylums, and in the founding of many additional jails and almshouses conducted on a reformed plan. She became interested in the condition of the insane abroad. Her work resulted in major reforms throughout the world.

As Miss Dix's work gradually extended the healing for the mentally ill around the world, Horace Mann said that he came "to Worship her divine prowess," and would have counted it happiness enough "to be the lackey of her bidding."

Samuel Gridley Howe, a student at Brown in Mann's day as a tutor, had come back to Boston, and now mutual interests drew him close to Mann. Howe had deserted medicine after graduating from Harvard Medical School in 1824, and had gone to fight with the Greeks for their independence. He had been imprisoned in Prussia as a champion of the Poles while in Europe investigating what was being done there for the blind. Now he wanted and intended to free blind children. He was prepared to give his own money and to go out and ask others for money for any cause in which he believed. He began in a small way to receive a few blind children at his father's house on Pleasant Street. In January of 1833, the project received help from the state Legislature, which voted $6,000 a year (later increased to $30,000) to his institution on condition that it educate without cost 20 poor blind from Massachusetts. Colonel Thomas H. Perkins, a prominent Bostonian, presented his mansion and grounds for the school.

The story of Dr. Howe's work in freeing the blind was much the same as the story of Horace Mann's fight for the hospital for the insane, although Howe's project was never at the beginning regarded with the same suspicion. Howe was better known in Boston, for one thing, and he had already proved his money-raising ability. Also, he had some money of his own to put into the fight, and he could win almost anybody to his side. The building which Colonel Perkins had presented to Howe for the school for the blind was found unsuitable, and Perkins consented to its sale, so that the institution could be moved to a large building in South Boston, which had previously been a fashionable hotel. It was henceforth known as the Perkins Institute for the Blind, the first school of its kind in the world.

Just when Howe and Mann became close friends is not important. They may have known each other at Brown, but Howe had been out of the country through many decisive years in Mann's life. Now in Boston, their mutual interests in progress drew them together. Mann visited the school for the blind many times, and was eventually made one of its trustees.

Howe's teaching methods enthralled Mann. Howe had investigated what was being done in Europe, but he had his own way of going about things. He always believed that there was no method that could not be improved upon.

One of his most famous pupils was Laura Bridgman, a child who had had her sight and hearing permanently destroyed by scarlet fever when she was two years of age. She entered the Perkins Institute in 1837. Dr. Howe at once set himself to teach her the alphabet by touch. He first pasted labels on several common articles—keys, spoons, knives— with the names of the articles in raised letters. As soon as she had learned all the names in this fashion, she was taught the individual letters, and gradually learned the alphabet and the ten digits.

A man is known by the company he keeps. Horace Mann had a special ability for making and keeping friends. He could recognize worth in others; he could respect their achievements; he could listen to what they had to say. He gave his love to those who, like himself, had given their love to humanity.

It was ordained by Elizabeth Peabody that Horace Mann should know Dr. W. E. Channing. It could not possibly have been otherwise after Elizabeth Peabody got to know Mann. She believed in heroes, and Channing was one of her greatest. Respecting, even loving Mann, she had to bring them together. She took Mann to call on Dr. Channing in 1833, and then sat down to record their conversation.

They agreed, she said, that human life on earth needs education. Mann thought that the State should regulate the sale of liquor, as it did more universally acknowledged poisons. Channing agreed with this. Both men thought of slavery not as a national but a sectional problem. Both men thought the North should help slaveholders through the immediate expense of emancipation, as the English Antislavery Society was trying to do for the West Indian planters. Mann favored colonization in Africa for freed slaves. He thought that there they might cultivate rice and cotton. Dr. Channing did not agree with this. He agreed with William Lloyd Garrison that colonization was a snare. "A freed slave," he said, "only increases the demand for more slaves." Mann became a member of Dr. Channing's congregation.

When Mann departed from Dedham, he had given up

his seat in the Massachusetts House of Representatives. Now, in 1834, Horace Mann was persuaded by his friends to enter the race for State Senator from Boston on the Whig ticket.

Elizabeth wrote Mary, still in Cuba, that the "Whig senators have been all severally abused in the *Post*. One day an article appeared in *The Mercantile Journal* in defence of Mr. Mann, who had been denounced as a 'wild visionary,' a 'projector of lunatic asylums,' 'a pledged member of the Temperance Society'!!! It was written with much spirit and lamented that *in Boston* a man should be opposed on the ground of his *divine philanthropy*."

On the evening of November 7 before the election on the 10th, Elizabeth wrote Mary that she had been to Dr. Channing's. He "instantly began to speak of Mr. Mann, about whose election to the Senate he is greatly interested." That same evening there was a great Whig caucus in Faneuil Hall, and Charles Curtis, a noted Boston lawyer, gave a passionate defense of Horace Mann. Curtis said that Mann had been charged in the paper with two crimes—having projected a lunatic asylum was one. Curtis said Mann *had* projected it, and *erected* it, and proceeded to give the whole history of Mann's actions on the subject. He was applauded with uproar. The other crime for which the papers blamed Mann was that of his being the friend of temperance. For this, too, Curtis said, he glorified Mann.

On November 10, Mann was elected to the Senate by a majority of nearly 3,000.

Horace Mann wrote to his sister Lydia: "What pleases me especially in this matter is, that as soon as my nomination appeared in the papers, all the taverners, distillers, and grocers, or as we call them, retailers, entered into a league to defeat my election on the ground of my being a temperance man. They held public meetings at which I was denounced, and one of the morning newspapers, 'The Post,' (for the rum-party have a newspaper), opposed my election most strenuously, calling upon all rum-sellers to vote against me, and doing me the distinguished honor to say that if I were in the Senate, I should cause all the license laws to be repealed, and should enact others making the sale of ardent spirits a crime. This paper, moreover, stigmatized me as being a 'projector of Lunatic Hospitals,' etc. It so happened, however, that being a temperance man and a friend of the Insane was a recommendation to some people, if not to the Jackson party. . . . My friends often congratulate me for being abused by the Post."

Mary and Sophia Peabody returned from Cuba in the spring of 1835. Horace was in correspondence with both Elizabeth and Mary and saw them when he could. He had come to depend on their friendship.

In November, 1835, a little over a year after his election to the Senate, Horace Mann reported to Lydia. His labors for the present year were over politically, he said, and he had had an arduous time in the Senate. He had been appointed Chairman of the Committee for the Revision of the Statutes. "We have a body of Statute Law, now, not surpassed, nor, as I believe, equalled in any other part of the world, for system, completeness, harmony, and perspicuity. I think I shall always look back upon this year's labor with satisfaction, and with a consciousness of having performed a service, which will live after me."

Mann had been reelected to the Senate, he told Lydia: "This fact, considering that I am so much a stranger in the city, is not without its gratification to me." His health was good, he said, and even improving.

He hoped to be home for Thanksgiving. He realized always what Lydia's devoted attendance on her mother had meant not only to their mother, but to all of them. He ended: "Our struggles can be but a short time longer—while it lasts, may we bear it as becomes us."

In March 6, 1837, Horace Mann said in a final paragraph of a letter to Mary Peabody that he had been to Franklin to see, "very probably for the last time upon earth, the best, most affectionate, and fondest of mothers. I found her very low, and she continued to fall." The physician, he said, had given up all hope for recovery. On March 19 of that year Rebecca Stanley Mann died at Franklin. In writing of his mother, Horace Mann said, "A memory full of proofs of the purest, strongest, wisest love is all that is left to me upon earth of a mother. . . . Death will not sanctify any of her precepts, her wise and judicious counsels; for they were sanctified and hallowed before."

Chapter 7

The Harvest Is Far Distant

On January 6, 1836, Mann was elected President of the Massachusetts Senate. As President, on April 20, 1837, he signed the act creating for the State of Massachusetts the first State Board of Education in the United States.

On May 4th of that year, Horace Mann was 41 years old. On that day, he began a journal, saying, "I have long had an inefficient desire to keep a journal. This desire has always been just at the most unlucky point,—so strong as to make me regret the omission, and yet too weak to induce me to supply it. . . . I wish to keep some remembrancer (daily when I am able, less frequently when I must) of the states of my mind, and of the most important transactions in which I may be concerned."

Some yeoman service to education had already been carried on in Massachusetts before the State Board of Education was made a fact. Such a board could never have been appointed if this work had not already been done. Of all the men who had worked to bring about the improvement of education in Massachusetts, the principal one was James G. Carter, a Harvard graduate and an experienced teacher.

In 1825, he had written a brilliant *Outline for an Institution for the Education of Teachers,* the base on which normal schools were later built. In 1837 he was chairman of the House Committee on Education, and it was Carter, with Mann's support as President of the Senate, who secured enactment of the bill creating the State Board of Education.

When the members of the first State Board of Education were announced, most of the names caused no surprise. Almost every man on the list had already proved his devotion to the cause of education. Although the majority of the men on the Board at the beginning were Unitarians and Whigs, the Board became orthodox later through replacements.

Governor Edward Everett, a Whig and Unitarian, was Chairman *ex officio,* and Lieutenant Governor George Hull, also a Whig and a Unitarian, was the other *ex officio* member. The other Board members were: James G. Carter, like Mann a Whig and Unitarian; the Reverend Emerson Davis, a Whig, pastor of the Congregational Church (Trinitarian) in Westfield; Edmund Dwight of Boston, Whig and Unitarian, a wealthy merchant and sponsor of Mann as Secretary of the Board; Horace Mann; the Reverend George Putnam of Roxbury, a Whig and pastor of the First Church (Unitarian) in Roxbury (he succeeded Mann as the Board's second Secretary); Edward A. Newton, a prominent Whig in Pittsfield and an Episcopalian; Robert Rantoul, Jr., of Gloucester, a leading Democrat in the Legislature and a Unitarian; the Reverend Thomas Robbins of Rochester, a Whig and pastor of the Congregational Church (Trinitarian) in Mattapoisett village in the town of Rochester; and the Reverend Jared Sparks, Whig and Unitarian, a historian who was to become President of Harvard.

One move caused great surprise. The majority of the educators of the state expected Carter to be made Secretary of the Board. When the position was offered to Mann, not only surprise but dismay was expressed.

Edmund Dwight persuaded Governor Everett to offer tht appointment to Mann. As a businessman, it seemed to Dwight a good idea to get a man who knew the laws of the state thoroughly, who had already proved his administrative abilities, and who had the capacity to carry on the enormous load of work to be done. Also, he said, it would be well to choose for the Board's executive officer a member of a profession other than teaching so that he could see the total picture. It was obvious from the beginning that there was much about the teaching profession that was going to have to be changed.

Whatever James Carter thought of the appointment, he remained loyal and cooperative.

On June 28, 1837, Mann received a call from Edmund Dwight on the subject of the Secretaryship. On June 29, Mann decided to take it and on June 30 he did. He was now no longer merely a member of the Board. He stood in a new relationship to the Board. "Nor to them only: I stand in a new relation to the world. . . . The harvest is far distant from the seedtime. *Faith* is the only sustainer. I have faith in the improvability of the race,—in their accelerating improvability. . . . "

July 1, "I mean soon to commence reading and writing with express reference to the office."

July 3. "What strikes me as most extraordinary in relation to my new office is, that every man, with the single exception of Dr. Channing, inquires concerning the *salary*, or makes remarks that look wholly to the comparative *honor* of the station; while no man seems to recognize its possible usefulness, or the dignity and elevation to which it is inwrought into beneficent action. . . . "

Dr. William Ellery Channing had written Mann, "I rejoice in it. . . . You could not find a nobler sphere. . . . Your willingness to consecrate yourself to this work is a happy omen."

One friend reproached him for giving up a successful law practice and a position of honor in the Senate to become a "post-rider from county to county looking after the welfare of children who will never know whence benefits may come and encountering the jealousy and prejudice and misrepresentation of ignorant parents."

Mann noted his reply to doubters in his journal: "If the title is not sufficiently honorable now, then it is clearly left for me to elevate it. I had rather be a creditor than debtor to the title."

Mann's income from his legal and legislative duties at this time was in excess of $3,000 a year. When he learned that the Legislature thought the job worth only $1,500 a year, and that his travel and office expenses must come from this, he said, "Well, one thing is certain: if I live and have health, I will be revenged on them; I will do them more than $1,500 worth of good."

Mann made his own job. He realized almost at once that he needed to know a great deal more about education than he then knew. He withdrew to the country, accordingly, and set himself a strict course of reading to find out for himself what were considered the best principles of education of the day. "My reading," he noted, "upon the subject of my duties is very delightful. Nothing could be more congenial to my tastes, feeling, and principles."

George Combe's *Constitution of Man,* published in 1828, had a profound effect upon Mann. He said that after reading it, he "ever after made it his textbook." He read James Simpson's work, *Necessity of Popular Education.* Maria Edgeworth's and Robert Lovell's two volumes, *Practical Education* he found "full of instruction. I have been delighted to find how often the views therein expressed had been written out on my own thinking. Had I ever read the book before, I should charge myself with unconscious plagiarism."

Mann was now well embarked upon his preparation of the case for his new client, "the next generation."

Whatever his concern for the new client, however, he soon learned that first he must win the new client's elders to his cause. He found them not only indifferent, lethargic, and uneasy at hearing what he had to tell them, but hostile as well. He decided to take his case for the next generation to the people of Massachusetts. Something had to be done, he felt, to make the public aware that the schools of Massachusetts were contributing nothing to the conception of liberty and equality for all, but were actually hindering it. The British idea of the class system persisted, even though a Revolution had been fought to assure the people of the United States a different world. The children of the wealthy classes attended private schools, and the children of the poor attended the district or township schools, which had increasingly low standards.

The struggle Horace Mann embarked upon was one that was singularly compatible with his temperament and beliefs. The battle to establish and improve the common or district schools, and to make them effective instruments for the education of the young people in a democracy, was to become one of the greatest struggles in American history. The first—and major—engagements were won during Horace Mann's day without bloodshed.

But the struggle still goes on. The reason for it, and the core of it, is whether all men, whether rich or poor, of whatever race or creed, have the right under the Constitution of the United States to have equal and integrated opportunities for education. Mann was determined to make the public schools of Massachusetts as good as schools could be made anywhere, so that the rich and poor could be educated equally, and so that there would be no dividing line between the educated and the ignorant because of circumstances beyond their control.

That Mann was not entirely without personal feelings in this matter is reflected in his journal. He had a long conversation with a man in Northampton who held that the British form of government with a monarch, Lords, and Commons, was the best in the world. This person, Horace Mann said, thought that social and economic classes were essential—one to work, the other to improve. "In the course of the conversation," Mann wrote, "he denied that the class he eulogized ever insulted those who started in life, as he would call it, below them; and yet he insulted me and all my relatives twice most outrageously. That is their way. Beginning with the principle that they are from their birth superior, they are constantly acting it out in life, embodying it in conduct, and yet profess to be ignorant that they are committing the grossest indignities."

Mann worked out a total plan for educating the people of Massachusetts about the conditions of their common schools, and the things that must be done to improve them.

As one part of this plan, he sent out circulars in August of 1837 announcing times and places for county meetings to which all people interested in education were invited. He thought he had made arrangements for these meetings to be well publicized, and for all interested people to be informed.

Mann set out on his tour with an address entitled "The Means and Objects of Common School Education" in his bag. He had collected his facts with care. He was determined to batter down the walls of citizen indifference. As a political speaker he had drawn together thousands of people. As an educator, he soon found he was fortunate in most places to attract a dozen people who really wanted to hear what he had to say.

He recorded in his journal some of his thoughts about the meetings, or county conventions, which he held during the first two years of his secretaryship. "To make an impression in Berkshire in regard to the schools," he wrote, "is like attempting to batter down Gibraltar with one's fist." After a meeting in Springfield, he observed, "If there is not more life in the body than in the head, it will soon decompose." Following a meeting at Northampton, he wrote: "Ah me! I have hold of so large a mountain that there is much danger that I shall break my own back in trying to lift it." He said of Barnstable, "I will work in this moral, as well as physical sandbank of a county until I get some new things to grow out of it." In Dedham, his former home, where he himself had served many times on the

Mann and Governor Briggs set up the Pittsfield meeting.

school board and where he had every reason to believe
that interest in education was high, he found the meeting
to be "a meager, spiritless, discouraging affair. . . . Surely
if the schoolmaster is abroad in this country I should be
glad to meet him." At Pittsfield, no arrangements had been
made to prepare the schoolhouse for a meeting. Mann and
Governor Briggs had to sweep the building, make the fire,
and set the furniture in order.

However discouraged Mann may have been, the sta-
tistics he had gathered kept him moving onward, and as
usual, he used the facts he had gathered as weapons. With
them, he felt sure he could eventually cut through the morass
of public apathy and demolish the enemies of education.

During 1837, the year Mann began his first tour, over
300 Massachusetts schools were broken up by mutinous pupils
or through the incompetence of teachers. The teachers of

the state had an average age of 16 years. The usual pay for a male teacher was $10 to $12 a month, and for a female teacher, $4 to $10, with the teacher boarding around. Severity in a teacher was considered a virtue. The schoolhouse in Sunderland, built in 1793, had a whipping post set firmly in the floor. Floggings were not the exception, but the rule. As late as 1844, the Boston Survey Committee found floggings in a representative school of the city averaged 65 per day for 400 children.

During this period, Mann was frequently in touch with Mary and Elizabeth Peabody. Mary, upon learning of his new post, had written playfully, "I feel slighted that you did not ask advice from such a distinguished pedagoguest as myself." She said that she liked the change for him very much, and thought that the roaming life would do him good.

Certainly there was roaming. He went from town to town on horseback, by train, by wagon, in carriages, and in a little sailing boat to Cape Cod. Here he found a delightful change. The audiences, he said, were "attentive and goodly." At Edgartown, "delegates even from the Orknew Islands of Chilmark," were gathered to hear him.

On the island of Nantucket, the meeting cheered him as nothing else had done. "Every part of the meetinghouse was rammed, crammed, jammed." Even so, everyone who wanted to hear him could not get in, and he was forced to repeat his lecture. He was afraid his second lecture would be cabbage twice boiled, but the second audience was even more enthusiastic than the first.

It was not happenstance that caused Mann's lectures in Nantucket to be heard by such attentive audiences. A remarkable man, Cyrus Peirce, lived on Nantucket. He had prepared the way for Mann by the years of work in education he had done on Nantucket, and by his understanding of what Mann was trying to do. Peirce had directed a private academy on Nantucket after his graduation with honors from Harvard. He thought he wanted to become a minister, and after two years at the academy, had returned to Harvard to the Divinity School. After he became a minister, however, it did not take him long to discover that teaching, not preaching, was what he had to do. He returned to Nantucket and the academy. A wider vision, however, made him persuade the leading citizens of Nantucket to join with him in bringing about a total reorganization of the school system there, from the primary school through the high school.

At the time Mann and Peirce met, Peirce had given up his private school and was Principal of the public Nantucket High School. Mann and Peirce talked far into the night. When Mann left Nantucket, he took away with him as many of Peirce's ideas about education as he left of his own with Peirce. Again, Mann's ability to absorb ideas from others and to recognize dedication to humanitarian causes and education brought to his side a man who was not only to become an interested co-worker but a passionate disciple to Mann's ideas.

Salem was near the end of Mann's tour. There, Mary Peabody was teaching a small school for girls in her father's house. She attended the meeting with Mann, and later gave her account of it.

She said it was remarkable to see the apathy with which the meeting opened. "One gentleman, who made one of the first speeches, questioned the expediency of endeavoring to get the educated classes to patronize public schools. He spoke, he said, in the interest of mothers who preferred private schools for their children; and he believed the reasons that they had for this would always prevail: they would have their children grow up in intimacies with those of their own class. No one spoke on the *American* side of this question. . . . No generous sentiment was touched."

Another man present said that before any other work was done by the State Board of Education, the Secretary should go about the state, spending a day in every public school in it. Only then, apparently, would the Secretary know what he was talking about. Mann said in reply that "if the gentleman who made the last proposition would take the trouble to do a short sum in arithmetic, he would find that it would take sixteen years for the Secretary to do this work, if he never intermitted one day."

"A general stir in the assembly," wrote Miss Peabody, "intimated that suddenly the immensity of the work to be done struck in their minds for the first time. . . ."

Mann found the meeting "one of the poorest."

Mann spoke at another meeting in Salem the next night. He had been invited by Silas Holbrook's Lyceum Lecture Bureau to address a meeting of the Lyceum system, for a fee, while in Salem for the school meeting. (Whenever possible, Mann combined paid lectures with free ones in order to defray his considerable expenses.) Mann had prepared a different lecture to be given to the Lyceum audience, but the officials of the Lyceum asked him to repeat the lecture on education of the night before. He did so, before a large audience, and it was an outstanding success.

There must have been many times during his speaking tours when Mann went to sleep puzzled as to why the same lecture would one time be a smashing success and another time a great failure. Was it his own temperament that made one lecture a success and the other a failure? Was it merely that some communities were more ignorant than others, less ready for his message? Was it fatigue? The mystery of the failure in Dedham, which was a lively and comparatively well educated community, and a community where thousands had listened to Mann previously, is most interesting.

Among other things that Mann said in the carefully prepared Dedham lecture, and that he repeated over and over, was this thought: "If the system of national instruction devised and commenced by Charlemagne had been continued, it would have changed the history of the French people. Such an event as the French Revolution could never have happened with free schools, any more than the American Revolution could have happened *without* them!

". . . Nothing is so good it cannot be made better—nothing so bad it might not become worse. . . . No community should rest content with being superior to other communities, while it is inferior to its own capabilities!. . ."

Mann returned to Boston in mid-November, and recorded in his journal: "My great circuit is now completed. The point to which, three months ago, I looked forward with so much anxiety, is reached. The labor is done. With much weariness, with almost unbounded anxiety, with some thwartings, but, on the whole, with unexpected and extraordinary encouragement, the work is done. That, however, is but the beginning. I confess, life begins to assume a value which I have not felt for five years before."

Chapter 8

One Step More

T oday," Mann recorded on November 16, 1837, "I have examined the returns in the Secretary's office, of which an abstract is to be made; and find they look very formidable. What an ocean of work lies before! Well, I am ready to plunge into it."

He began work on his first Report, ostensibly to the State Board of Education, but actually to the people of Massachusetts and the country at large. Of all Mann's writings on education, the 12 Annual Reports he wrote as Secretary of the Board are the most valuable. Together they fill 1,000 pages in his *Life and Works,* and in them he spells out his findings, his thoughts, and his recommendations about various educational matters. These reports did more than any other thing Mann wrote in arousing the people, not only of Massachusetts but of the United States, to the necessities for reform and changes in education. The Reports were widely circulated, quoted, and read, abroad as well as in the United States.

Of these Reports, George B. Emerson, head of a private school for girls in Boston, said, "They are echoing in the woods of Maine and along the St. Lawrence and the Lakes. They are heard throughout New York and throughout all the West and Southwest. A conviction of their importance has sent a Massachusetts man to take charge of the schools of New Orleans: they are at this moment regenerating those of Rhode Island. In the remotest corner of Ohio 40 men, not children and women, but *men* meet together to read aloud a single copy of the Secretary's Reports which one of them receives; thousands of the best friends of humanity of all sects, parties, and creeds in every State of the Union are familiar with the name of Horace Mann."

The subjects of the Reports form a rollcall of Mann's beliefs and interests, some of them dating back to his childhood:

The duties of school committees, especially in the selection of teachers; the modernization of schoolhouses; the teaching of reading by the word-method rather than by single letters; the responsibility of the people for the improvement of schools; the formation of good reading habits and the need for the establishment of public schools; the necessity of abolishing the district schools and of providing unified ones; the contribution of education to industry and science; the need for a practical course of study to prepare students for daily living; the value of the study of physiology and hygiene; the importance of oral instruction, elementary science, language exercises, geography built upon the life around students, music, and drawing; a comparison of teaching methods in European schools with those of Massachusetts' schools; the value of normal schools and teachers' institutes for the better training of teachers; the necessity of equal educational opportunities for all children; the

[97]

relation of education to crime; the urgent need for deliberately educating young people for life in a democracy.

Mann's Reports are important records of the progress of his thinking about education and his increasing knowledge of the subject. They are, in a sense, his public journal of accomplishment. They are frequently moving, often impassioned, and are basic to any study of the American public school system.

But they were, for Mann, only one more way of educating the public. It seemed to him that he must lay his hands on everything at once. There could be no resting place. His first tour of the state had shown him so many abuses to be corrected and changes to be made that he charged in several directions with almost frenzied energy.

His personal life took a turn for the better. He had paid off the debts contracted by his brother, Stanley, and on November 29, 1837, he was able to leave the office where he had slept for three lonely years, grieving for Charlotte, sometimes hardly knowing where to turn. "May I not hope," he asked himself, "that at least the privations of which I have been subject in this place may not continue to visit me at another residence?"

Thanksgiving Day, 1837, he spent alone, hard at work on his Report. He had written to sister Lydia in Franklin, "Your Thanksgiving will not be like the last for Mother will not be there. The circle grows smaller. The friends are assembling in another place. We have some duties to perform or we should not be left."

He went about his personal life in a characteristic way. He attended a meeting in Faneuil Hall one night protesting mob violence against the Abolitionists. Through a sense of duty, he attended a party given by a newly elected mayor. He listened to Emerson's lectures. The third lecture he heard Emerson give, he noted, was "not so lucid, pellucid, as the others. . . . 'Have a room by yourself,' said Emerson, according to Mann's report. 'If you cannot without, sell your coat and sit in a blanket.' " He dined with the Lorings. He attended meetings called by Dr. Channing to find out what sort of world they were living in, what influences predominated in society, what was wrong, and what means could be devised to set the wrong right. Dr. Channing's remarks had perspicuity and distinctness that his mind imparted to whatever it handled.

On the last day of the year, Mann re-read his first Report, which he had just finished for presentation to the Board the following day. He was tired, but could still note about his work as Secretary that "severe as this labor is, it is surrounded by the most delightful associations."

In January he began his work on his Schoolhouse Report, from which he hoped beautiful schoolhouses would grow—a whole crop of them. (The seed was well planted, for in the ten years following Mann's Report, the sums raised by the self-taxation of the several districts, towns, and cities in the state, and spent for the building or repairing of schoolhouses alone was $2,200,000, considerably more than all the money that had been spent on schoolhouses in all the years before the Report.)

Mann was asked to speak before the House of Representatives, and said that he was able to hold a pretty full house for an hour and a half, "stiller and stiller to the end."

Early in February, he held a meeting that he found full of interest and promise to all the teachers of the primary schools of Boston. The idea of having teachers of the same grades meet together once a week to hear a lecture on education, or to exchange views with one another, was an idea that was dear to him. Future meetings, it seemed to Mann, promised much in behalf of the children of the city.

Always with him was another idea he felt he had to put into action if education was to be improved in Massachusetts, training institutes and normal schools for teachers. Unless teachers could get more and better training, their instruction would not be improved. And unless their instruction was improved, the quality of education in the state could not be changed.

On the night of March 10, 1838, Mann went to a meeting at the home of State Board of Education member Edmund Dwight; and once again, a meeting with Dwight produced results. Now Dwight gave Mann authority to propose to the Legislature, in Mann's own way, that $10,000 should be forthcoming from Dwight or others, provided the Legislature would give the same amount, the total sum to be used for establishing teachers seminaries.

Dwight gave his support—financial and otherwise—to Mann at every turn. Greatly interested in education, his home became the center of meetings to promote the common schools; and for many years, hardly a step was taken relating to that subject without his consultation and advice.

On March 13, Mann had the satisfaction of reporting this gift, which Dwight had specified was to be anonymous, to the President of the Massachusetts Senate and to the Speaker of the House. "This appears to be glorious!" Mann wrote. "I think I feel pretty sublime! Let the stars look out for my head!" Although the first public normal school was not to be opened for more than two years, the first major step had now been taken to assuring adequate training for the teachers of the state.

There was never, however, a resting place for Mann in his battle to put life into the schools of Massachusetts. He decided that he must have a method of communicating directly and regularly with the teachers of the state. Accordingly, he inaugurated the *Common School Journal* as a private enterprise. Published twice a month, each number contained 16 pages, making an annual volume of 384 pages. The subscription price was $1 a year.

On November 17, 1838, Mann was able to set down in his journal that on that day the first issue of the *Common School Journal* had appeared. "With this," he wrote, "I hope to awaken some attention to the great subject I have in hand. . . . I know it will involve great labor; but the results at the end, not the labor at the beginning, are the things to be regarded."

Great labor it did involve, since Mann wrote many of the issues completely by himself. The *Journal* continued for 14 years, 10 of them under Mann's editorship, and it answered its purpose. It contained some of Mann's best thoughts on education, and also the Annual Reports in condensed form. Lists of words frequently mispronounced or misspelled appeared in it. Some of its aphorisms are reminiscent of Benjamin Franklin's *Poor Richard's Almanac*. Everything that Mann wrote and published in the *Common School Journal*, as elsewhere, was directed to improving education and the human race.

Here are samples from the *Common School Journal*:

[*101*]

" 'Why, Neighbor Simple,' said Mr. Farsight, one bright morning, when Mr. Simple was mowing a lot, where the grass stood so thin that the spires looked lonesome, 'Why, Neighbor Simple, you had a fine lot here with a strong soil, but your blades of grass are so far apart, that they might grow into hoop-poles and not crowd each other.'

" 'Yes,' said Mr. Simple, 'I've been thinking I was almost a fool, for I ought to have sowed a bushel of good hay-seed upon this piece, but the truth is, I bought only a peck and so I scattered it about so much the thinner, and now I see I have lost a ton of hay by it.'

"Well," said Mr. Farsight, "don't you think you were about as near being a fool when you voted, last town meeting, against granting any more school money for sowing the seeds of knowledge in the minds of the children, as you were when you scattered a peck of hay-seed where you ought to have sowed a bushel? Now, remember, Neighbor Simple, what I tell you; next year, wherever there is not grass in this lot, there'll be weeds.' "

"In the Annual Report, just presented to the Legislature, of the Board of Inspectors of the State Prison at Charlestown, we find the following:

" 'THE TIME IS NOT VERY DISTANT, WHEN, FROM THE INCREASING POPULATION OF THE COMMONWEALTH, AN ADDITION TO THE ACCOMMODATIONS OF THE PRISION WILL BE REQUIRED.'

"Yes, Honorable Legislators! If you do not improve the schools, you must enlarge the prisons.

"Who dares to say that, of the *three hundred and*

eighteen souls in that weeping and wailing, or cursing and blaspheming company, in the State Prison, there are so many as fifty, who, with proper early education, would not have been useful, honorable, happy members of society?"

"It is an arrangement of Providence, as beautiful as it is wise, that children are brought into the world *without habits.* Through these, the educator can make the child better than himself."

"**If Adam** had named 'all cattle and the fowl of the air and every beast of the field' without seeing them, think you he would have known which was which, when he actually saw them afterwards? So it is when children read words, without understanding their meaning."

"Lost, yesterday, somewhere between sunrise and sunset, two golden hours, each set with sixty diamond minutes. No reward is offered for they are gone forever."

On July 3, 1839, the first normal school in the world, devoted exclusively to the training of women as teachers, was opened in Lexington, Massachusetts. Mann had persuaded Cyrus Peirce to leave Nantucket and take over the directorship of the school. Fifteen hundred dollars seemed to be a magic figure to the Legislature, for Peirce, too, was offered that salary. Without a backward glance, he gave up the security and prestige that he had won on Nantucket for the precariousness of the new venture. Mann himself mortgaged his law library and later sold it to get the money to keep the Lexington school going.

He was at Lexington, of course, for the opening of the school. "The day opened," he recorded, "with one of the most copious rains we have had this rainy season. Only three persons presented themselves for examination for the Normal School. In point of numbers, this is not a promising commencement. How much of it is to be set down to the weather, how much to the fact that the opening of the school has been delayed so long, I cannot tell." He added a characteristic note, "What remains but more exertion, more and more, until it *must* succeed?"

More students were to present themselves, and by September 9, Cyrus Peirce was able to report that the school had 12 scholars: "They seem industrious and interested; and nearly every one of *fair* capacity. But many of them are yet backward." Peirce's observations, however optimistic he might be, led him to acknowledge that his young ladies were greatly deficient in reading and spelling.

At the beginning of the second term, Mann enrolled his nieces, Rebecca Pennell, then 18, and her younger sister Eliza, 17. With no children of his own, Mann had always taken special interest in the progress of these girls; and now he intended to see that they got the kind of higher education few young women of that day could secure. The girls were earnest, hardworking, and determined that they would be credits to their uncle and justify his belief in them. They repaid him fully for his help in the way he appreciated most: both became excellent teachers.

The Lexington normal school was but the first of three which the Board of Education had decided to establish—one in the northeastern, one in the southeastern, and one in the western parts of the state. They were to be conducted for three years as experiments. The funds for them were inadequate, and the Board asked for the cooperation of various towns in furnishing buildings, land, and even services. The towns responded to the request with varying degrees of enthusiasm. After Lexington had been chosen as the first location for a school for young ladies only, Barre was chosen as the second site for a school for both sexes. The Lexington school was moved twice before it found a final home at Framingham. The Barre school was also moved once, to Westfield. The third normal school founded under Mann's Secretaryship was established at Bridgewater, and remained there.

A storm against Mann's efforts on behalf of educational reform was beginning to gather. Schoolmasters who had been going along on the theory that what had been good enough for grandfather was good enough for grandson now saw that Mann intended to change all this. Orthodox church leaders saw that he meant business about separating the church and the state in the schools. Wherever there were special interests that Mann attacked, there was special resistance to his work—and much of this resistance came from the poor and ignorant, whom he was trying to help, because they could not read his speeches, could not understand his words, and could not comprehend what he was trying to do.

The very urgency with which he attacked the evils and corruption of the entrenched school system, where there was no equality of opportunity, was what won him success in the end. He was determined to have an educational system in the United States that was universal, nonsectarian, free, and aimed at social efficiency, civic virtue, and character.

He was determined that there would be no differences in the education offered a student, whether rich or poor. Eventually Mann became equally convinced that there should be no differences in the education offered students, whatever differences there might be in creed or race. One step forward, for Mann, always had to be followed by one step more. He was a logical man. He was a sane man. The sensitivity produced by his own suffering became a social force to help reduce the suffering of others.

Chapter *9*

Two Journeys

In 1838 Mann had moved to establish district libraries for the schools. He began searching for books that would interest and instruct young people.

Elizabeth Peabody recommended Nathaniel Hawthorne's *Twice-Told Tales* to him. Mary Peabody thought that a manuscript of her mother's, *The Story of the Pilgrims,* would be suitable for school libraries, and she wrote to Mann to suggest it. Other people, too, suggested books; and Mann was sometimes so outspoken in his objections that he managed to offend a number of people, including some orthodox ministers, who believed that he had rejected one book, *A Child at Home,* because it was too religious in tone. Actually, Mann's letter to the book agent, Frederick A. Packard, who had offered the book to him, said that he was rejecting it because there was scarcely anything in the book that presented God in an admirable or loving aspect.

Packard concealed his anger, and offered Mann two other books, a primer and a spelling book. Mann found the primer filled with tales of horrifying fates that overtook wicked little boys and girls. With his memory of the horrors he had suffered as a child because of Dr. Emmons' interpretation of wickedness, he had no difficulty in rejecting that book. The spelling book was too old-fashioned, he thought, and showed no knowledge of recent findings about the teaching of spelling. Packard became an implacable enemy of Horace Mann, and set about getting the organized opposition of the orthodox clergy to Mann as Secretary of the Board.

Mann was under great pressures during 1838, and he must frequently have been near the breaking point.

During that year—and it could not have been at a better time—George Combe came into Mann's life. Combe, a Scotsman, a lawyer, and a phrenologist, was greatly interested in education and in the treatment of the criminal classes and the insane. He had written *Constitution of Man*, which Mann had taken as his "textbook" earlier. Combe probably had the greatest influence upon Mann of any man in his life. In 1838 Combe was invited to give a series of lectures in America.

On September 30, Mann set down in his journal: "Yesterday was the anniversary of my marriage. I had been much overcome by the unusual labors of the week and the brightness and the gloom associated with this anniversary forbid even my noticing the day with a written memento of its passage. Peace, beautitude, ever be thine, my dearest wife, while I mournfully sojourn in this vale of tears." But on October 8, a brighter note came into the journal. Mann noted that he had that day been introduced to George Combe, Esq., of Edinburgh; two days later he was accompanied to a convention by Mr. and Mrs. Combe.

The personal qualities of these two men and their

mutual belief in the improvability of the human race were bound to draw them together. What interested Mann most of all in Combe's writings, lectures, and conversation was his philosophy of human nature and human development. Mann became Combe's devoted disciple and supporter.

The "science" of phrenology has become so discredited today that it is not possible to say that Mann and Combe believed in it without somehow seeming to discredit them. But many people believed with Combe and Mann that the bumps on human craniums represented their various mental capacities. That Mann himself was not primarily concerned with phrenology is shown by a letter he wrote his sister Lydia in November, 1838. He said he intended to send her a copy of Combe's *Constitution of Man:* "I want you to read something on Phrenology," he said, "not that you may become a believer in that part of it which treats the correspondence between the powers of the mind and the external development of the head, but that you may study thoroughly and become complete master of that system of mental philosophy which is maintained by the phrenologists. . . . I know of no book, written for hundreds of years, which does so much to 'vindicate the ways of God to man,' as does the *Constitution of Man.*"

Combe's belief that the Golden Rule was the central principle of religion appealed to Mann. Combe's belief that illness was not a punishment of God for man's sins but an ignorance on the part of man of God's laws for healthy living did much to improve Mann's own health and mental attitude. Both men could agree that every child should be given the means for finding self-improvement, and that no self-improvement was vital that did not ally itself consciously with the improvement of others. Combe, said Mann, seemed to understand far better than any other man he ever saw the principles on which the human race has been formed, and by following which the most sure and rapid advancement could be secured. Mann had never met anyone "with a mind which handled such great subjects with such ease, and, as it appears . . . with such justness."

About Mann, Combe wrote that he "is a delightful companion and friend and among all the excellent men whom we met with at Boston, none entwined themselves more deeply and closely with our affections."

Early in August of 1839, at a time when Mann would usually have been mourning the death of Charlotte, the Combes persuaded him to visit them in Portland, Maine. Mann was much worn, Combe said, and Combe remonstrated with him on his disobedience to the laws of health that Mann was supposed to be teaching.

Mann's realization of the battle for the schools his opponents were beginning to organize against him can be judged by Combe's account:

Mann "told me that he is engaged in establishing normal schools, and the opposition is such that he had been exhausted in meeting it. . . . There are five thousand teachers in Massachusetts, and to say that normal schools are necessary is resented by them as a personal insult on their qualifications. There are many authors and publishers interested in the existing school books; to say that they are ill adapted for instruction is to affect their interest and render them enemies. There are numerous sectarian clergymen, and to expound a principle in morals or physiology which they think dangerous rouses their hostility. . . . To shape his course so as to disarm this formidable host of opponents, and yet persevere in improving schools, school books, and teachers, is a difficult, anxious, and laborious task, and he has scarcely any mental support. He is resolved to sacrifice both health and life, if necesssary, to the great cause, and will die at his post, if he is not dismissed from it for doing his duty. I have sympathized with him, encouraged him, and endeavored to induce him to take means of improving his health. He is invaluable to Massachusetts."

Mann told Combe that his effectual aid had advanced Mann's labors by years. Certainly Combe improved Mann's health by making him realize that his deliberate overwork was not good either for his efforts or his physical and mental well-being.

In March 1840, Mann recorded in his journal that "the bigots and vandals" in the Legislature were "signally defeated in their wicked attempts to destroy the Board of Education: 182 in favor of the attempt, 245 against it." Letters of congratulation came from some of the most influential men in the land. Mann felt that he needed and deserved a rest from the battles for the public schools, and he "struck up a bargain" with the Combes to travel West with them to Ohio. The Combes wanted to see something of the United States before returning to England, and Mann realized that his ignorance of the geography of his own country was quite as great as theirs.

With the Combes, Mann left New York on March 25, 1840, going by rail to Philadelphia, Baltimore, and Washington, and then on to Frederick, Maryland, by another railroad. From Frederick to Cessna, Pennsylvania, they traveled by private carriage; from Cessna to Little Crossings to Brownsville, Pennsylvania, over the National Road to Wheeling, now in West Virginia, by stage. At Wheeling, they took a river boat to Cincinnati, visiting General William Henry Harrison at North Bend, Ohio, then sailing on down the Ohio to Louisville, Kentucky. From Louisville, they again took a carriage to Frankfort, Lexington, and Maysville, Kentucky, where Mann stayed on for a while, while the Combes returned to Cincinnati. Mann and the Combes rejoined each other in Pittsburgh. From there they proceeded by canal boat to Johnstown. They took a portage railroad to Hollydaysburg, a canal boat again to Harrisburg, Pennsylvania, and a train from Harrisburg to Philadelphia. Green wood, burned on the train to Philadelphia, "clogged the flue, and the train jumped the track once." They went on from Philadelphia to New York, and Mann finally ended his tour on May 5, 1840, in Boston.

"I am satisfied," wrote Mr. Mann, "that the only way to get an adequate idea of this country is to travel through it. No imagination can give the realizing sense of its vastness, which is caused by that deepening, day after day, of the impression made by actually seeing it, and by combining the two elements of rapidity and length of time in passing over it. The imagination may conceive of great extent in an hour, or even in a minute: but imagination cannot hold on day after day; and all her impressions upon the brain do not leave traces so vivid, deep, and strong as come from actual observation, and from being made to comprehend by seeing and feeling, suffering and enjoying."

His trip was both "agreeable and instructive."

Mary and Elizabeth Peabody, with whom Mann had maintained a friendship by correspondence and visits since they had boarded together at Mrs. Clarke's, came back into his life more immediately in the summer of 1840. Mann was a frequent visitor at a bookshop Elizabeth had opened up on West Street in Boston. There she held forth in what was to become Boston's liveliest center for young intellectuals with new and untried ideas. At one time or another most of the leading intellectuals of Boston came to the bookshop—Emerson, George Bancroft, Bronson Alcott, George Ripley, Hillard, Dr. Channing, Washington Allston. There Margaret Fuller gave her Conversations; there Jones Very occasionally read his sonnets to a few of the chosen.

Elizabeth had moved the whole family to Boston. She and her mother imported and sold foreign books. Mrs. Peabody worked on a translation of Goethe's *Hermann und Dorothea*. In the midst of all the ferment, Mary Peabody and her father went about their own business: he helped some in the shop and also ran his own small shop on the ground floor, where he sold homeopathic medicines. Mary was a teacher first and last. Like the German, Friederich Froebel, she was passionately interested in what happened to children before they were old enough to enter school. She had founded a kindergarten in the same year he had opened his kindergarten abroad. She worked some in the shop, but had her little pupils in the mornings, and in the afternoons she taught French and drawing lessons. She was at work on a geography, which was to come out in installments in the *Common School Journal*.

Horace Mann came to the shop with increasing frequency. He found in the family an underpinning of belief in his work for education that gave him strength to carry out his own revolutionary ideas. He found in Mary an educated woman with a belief in the eternal educability of man as dedicated as his own. Mann needed an underpinning of faith, for it seemed that he hardly had time to conclude one battle before it was time for the next.

Not all, however, was dark. Mann wrote to Combe in February of 1842 that he had just finished his fifth Annual Report: "A bill is now pending before the Legislature to grant further aid for the continuance of the Normal schools, and to encourage, by a small bonus, the respective districts of the State to purchase a small school-library. We have pretty strong hopes that it will pass. . . . "

On March 3, he records the triumph in his journal: "The brightest days which have ever shone upon our cause were yesterday and to-day. Yesterday, resolves passed the House for granting $6,000 per year for three years to the Normal schools; and fifteen dollars to each district for a school-library, on condition of its raising fifteen dollars for the same purpose.

"Language cannot express the joy that pervades my soul. . . ."

By March 15th, his joy was not yet exhausted, for on that day he wrote to his niece Rebecca: "I am in pretty good health, and in *dangerous* spirits. Our triumph in the Legislature was magnificent. I am keeping perpetual jubilee. . . . Never was anything more triumphant. Eighteen thousand dollars for the Normal schools, and more than $30,000 for the Library. No change in parties or politics can get this out of our hands."

[*114*]

The Peabodys rejoiced with Mann. The Peabodys had other causes for rejoicing. On July 9, 1842, Sophia Peabody was married to Nathaniel Hawthorne in the West Street book-parlor. Sophia was 33 at the time, Mary was 36, and Elizabeth was 38.

In less than a year, Mary, too, was married. On March 26, 1843, Horace Mann set down in his journal: "This day of my life . . . I have engaged myself to be married to Miss Mary T. Peabody, a lady whose noble and elevated character, whose just and pure sentiments, whose capacities and attainments, and whose unfathomed depth of affection have long since won my admiration and my love."

"Circumstances," wrote Mann, "have hitherto rendered it improper that I should avow my secret affection for her, but certain affairs of my life are approaching such a crisis that it could not well be delayed longer without being smothered forever. I have projected a voyage to Europe in company with Dr. Howe and we propose to sail next month. I have felt as tho' it would be too painful to go and leave so lovely a being and one in whom I had such an interest, behind me. The voyage will be of tenfold pleasure and service to us in company; and it will promote my ulterior views which are concentrated upon advancing the great work of education. In this cause, I know the object of my affection will be of the greatest help I could possibly have. . . ."

Horace Mann and Mary Peabody were married on May Day, 1843, again in the book-parlor at West Street. Again, as it had on Sophia's wedding day, it rained, this time a torrential downpour throughout New England. Sophia, Miss Lydia Mann, Mrs. Rebecca Mann Pennell, Rebecca and Eliza Pennell—none could get to the wedding. It did not matter. Mary wore a plain white grasscloth gown with a small piece of embroidery about her throat; her one ornament was a gold chain band around her head, a gift of Horace Mann. Elizabeth went with them to the Cunard docks and saw them aboard the *Britannia*.

The newlyweds' traveling companions, Samuel and Julia Ward Howe, together with Julia's 17-year-old sister, Annie Ward, were already on board. Julia, the witty and lovely daughter of a wealthy New York banker, with illustrious ancestors and a warm and romantic heart, had fallen in love with Howe, who was 18 years older, during the summer of 1842 when she was visiting near Boston. Charles Sumner, who was regarded by Sam Howe as the brother of his heart, and Longfellow, another friend of Howe's, had called on Julia in Boston, and had told her much of Howe and his great achievements in educating the blind. She asked to see the Perkins Institute, and Sumner took her there. Howe, for his part, saw and fell in love with Julia. He insisted on an early marriage. Samuel Howe and Julia Ward had been married four days before the *Britannia* set sail, and Julia and Mary met for the first time on that voyage.

The first days at sea were rough and uncomfortable. Julia gave a brief picture of the voyage in a letter she wrote her sister, Louisa: "I have had two days of extreme suffering. . . To-day I am on deck, able to eat soup and herring, with grog in small doses. Husband very kind, takes good care of me. I am good for nothing, but try to be courageous. Mr. and Mrs. Mann are very loving. . . . Mrs. Mann wrote to me yesterday, and recommended lemonade. I wrote back to her and recommended leeks and onions. . . ."

[*116*]

The Britannia *battled through heavy seas.*

Mann recorded in a letter to his sister Rebecca that the sea was "pretty rough." Mary, he said, was the only live lady in the ship the first day. Dr. Howe had a special prescription for seasickness: "You must not tell the Tee-to-tallers that we have all drunk brandy all around this morning but we considered ourselves out of the jurisdiction of the American Temperance Society and under the law of Neptune and Nations."

In London, the Howes and Manns took lodgings at Number 31 Upper Baker Street. Mary wrote Elizabeth that when she and Horace had shut the door of their rooms and sat down alone together for the first time, it gave her a little bit of home feeling. "The only evil in my lot, thus far, has been this living in public. When I am married to Mr. Mann the next time I will not go on board a steamer immediately but retire into the country for a time. . . ."

Mann had gone abroad to study the schools and prisons of Europe so that he might further improve those of Massachusetts. On that trip he probably saw the inside of more prisons and asylums than anyone else in the world except Dorothea Dix. And Mary accompanied him.

The Howes and Manns lived very different lives in England. Charles Dickens had written about the Institute of the Blind in his *American Notes,* and all the great and famous wanted to meet Howe. But Howe was a reformer, too, and he wanted to see as many asylums and work-houses as he could. Charles Dickens made it possible for Howe, with Mann accompanying him, to investigate many of the darker places of London to which they could not have safely gone alone.

One of Dicken's notes to Howe tells how these expeditions were arranged: "My dear Howe,—Drive to-night to St. Giles's Church. Be there at half-past 11—and wait. One of Tracey's people will put his head into the coach after a Venetian and mysterious fashion, and breathe your name. Follow that man. Trust him to the death.

"So no more at present from

The Mask."

Ninth June, 1843

Chapter **10**

The World Abroad

Mary and Horace Mann were not impressed by what they saw in England. The inequalities made Horace boil with indignation and rejoice that he was not an Englishman, Mary reported to Elizabeth.

Sights that filled others with admiration and awe filled him with distaste, even horror. The Manns visited Eaton Hall in Liverpool, one of the seats of the Marquis of West-minster. Mann found it only a massive pile. He reported that the gardens and pleasure grounds covered 52 acres—about the size of Boston Common—and that they apparently contained every variety of flower and plant and fruit that could be found on earth. He could take no pleasure in the sight because he also saw a dozen old women carrying upon their backs the limbs of a large tree that had been cut down. Over the whole estate, other poor women weeded the walks, gathered in the new-mown hay, and did other rough physical labor. The marble floor of the entrance hall that had cost $75,000 filled him with wonder as to why the same amount of money could not have been spent for a better purpose. The attendant showed them the young ladies' garden. Mann asked himself whether there was "no spot in the souls of these tenderly reared daughters where a brighter flower than any ever formed of rain and sunshine could have been cultivated—the flower of sympathy for others' hearts. . . ."

Mann's first impressions of the inequalities of life in England only deepened as they continued their travels. Splendor and squalor, wealth and poverty existed side by side. That such coexistence seemed not to be questioned by any one appalled him. On the other hand, Mann himself was an aristocrat of the intellect. He would have been hard put to it to defend his ideas of equality when he resented so fiercely the fact that he found people he thought truly great—Lord Mansfield, William Wilberforce, James Watt—placed side by side with kings and queens like "gold pieces among copper pennies." Deposited in the same structure with the remains of the poets, Ben Jonson, Milton, Dryden, Pope, and Addison, he said contemptuously, was "a sprinkling of ladies of the bed-chamber, masters of the hounds, pimps, etc., who obtained this resting place for their bones through favoritism."

He visited the Jews' quarter. He could not understand how it was possible for people to be forced to live in such ruins, without dignity, without hope, when on all sides of the quarter was so much "luxury, voluptuousness, and superflous wealth!"

Mann, of course, visited many schools, and talked about education with anyone who would talk with him on the subject. He was duly armed with the proper credentials and introductions, but preferred to walk into the schools unannounced because, Mrs. Mann said, he wished to see them in "undress," and therefore visited them unofficially whenever possible.

A factory commissioner told him that he had many times seen certificates signed by a cross given to children by school-teachers because the teachers were unable to write their own names. Mann found most of the schoolmasters and directors of schools upholding and teaching the doctrines of the Church of England because of their fear that they would be crushed by the Establishment if they did not.

At the National Training College, a normal school, he found that the land, building, and fixtures cost $103,000, but that only 60 pupils were to be educated there at any one time. "How enormous an outlay," he exclaimed, "for the object to be accomplished!" He approved of a school in Sharp Alley that was conducted on principles of toleration. This school, the City of London Royal British School for Boys, was open to boys of all religious faiths; and there Mann found in almost equal numbers, Churchmen and Dissenters, and also Roman Catholics and Jews.

At the Home and Colonial Infant-school, conducted on the principles of Johann Pestalozzi, Mann was told by John Reynolds, the principal, that nine-tenths of all the children in the kingdom got all the education they ever received before they were nine years of age.

At the Blue Coat School, the headmaster told Mann that he considered the teaching of morality a humbug: he taught religion, not morality. The headmaster thought it was nonsense to try to teach children the value of truth and the wrongness of falsehood, because Nature had taught all children to lie. "How strange it is," Mann set down in his journal, "that, on every other subject, the existence of reason is acknowledged: on that of religion, the most important of all, blind authority is appealed to!"

The children of London's poor depressed Mann most of all. He visited Norwood and saw more than a thousand children of parents who were in the London poorhouses. He saw the great numbers of children who were committed to Bridewell Prison. Some of the children, not more than 12 years of age, had been imprisoned there repeatedly before. He wrote: "There are certain quarters of London, where children are born, educated, trained to go to Bridewell . . . or to be hanged . . . as certainly as poultry are raised to be eaten."

Horace Mann was a man of deep humility. He had gone abroad, not to criticize, but to learn better ways of educating. He began his investigations in England with hope that turned to despair. The inequalities were mountainous; there was no coordinated course of study; teachers were for the most part poorly paid; the Church dominated the majority of the schools; the books were very poor in the lowest class of schools; and the schoolhouses—with the exception of the palaces of the privately owned or endowed schools— were inferior to those of Massachusetts.

Even at Oxford University, Mann found that scholarship was indifferent and that a full professor could fail to know that the United States had the same common law as England. At the great Bodleian Library, he found that books were assembled according to their sizes, rather than their subjects. Not only his republican upbringing and his belief in the dignity of man, but also his intelligence and his common sense made him reject most of what he saw.

The Manns found Scotland a relief after England. The

scenery they saw was magnificent, and Mann even allowed himself a day or two of recreation to climb a mountain and to visit Loch Lomond, which was "beautiful and grand."

He thought the schools were better than in England. The teachers did "not stand immovably fixed to one spot," nor were "the bodies of the pupils mere blocks of wood, resting immovably in their seats." The pupils, as a matter of fact, jumped to their feet "quickly and joyfully" when answering to a question. Mann was troubled by the fact that prizes were given to the best scholars, and that they were thus encouraged to work to outdo their classmates rather than themselves.

But Mann found in Scotland many of the same inequalities he had found in England. That they were not as great was because there was not so great wealth. The Duke of Buccleuch's dog-kennels were better built and more comfortable than half the cottages in England and Scotland. The poor districts of Glasgow, which Mann visited with the superintendent of police, were "inconceivably wretched." Again, the schools were Church-dominated.

Mann's thoughts were now turning more and more homeward, and to his seventh Annual Report in which he would be reporting not only the school systems he was investigating abroad, but also the prisons, workhouses, asylums, hospitals, and schools for the blind and the deaf. The six months' leave permitted for his travels abroad put a time pressure on him that kept him moving from school to school, asylum to asylum, with no rest anywhere. The fact that he was paying for the entire trip from his own savings put a financial pressure on him that was very great. Mary recorded sorrowfully that he was not well much of the time but could not allow himself the salvation of any recreation.

Mary and Horace Mann moved on to Ireland and then to the Continent.

In Hamburg they saw a park, planted with beautiful trees and shrubs and flowers, open to the public. The truant boy from the street and the day laborer as well as people of means had free access to it. Mann was amazed to find that no tree or shrub was ever injured, no flower ever picked. "Suppose the whole of Boston Common to be laid out like a gentleman's garden, the fences to be removed, and the whole thrown open to every one who might choose to enter, whether from the city or from the country: how long would the walks remain uninjured, the trees and plants unmutilated, the flowers unplucked? This is certainly a lesson to republican America."

The Manns had earlier looked forward to spending time in Scotland with the Combes. When they had arrived there, however, they found that Combe had been ordered to the Continent because of a lung ailment and that he had been condemned to silence by his physicians. Now, to the ·great joy of both Mann and Combe, they met unexpectedly in Leipzig. The two friends were told they must talk very little to one another; but they disregarded the orders, and talked from morning till night during the short time they had together. In spite of his friends' fears, Mary Mann said, Mr. Combe improved every day. "At last, time was no more for them; and they reluctantly parted, never to meet again on earth except in the affections, and in such measure of intellectual companionship as correspondence by letter could give."

The Manns and Howes had intended to join each other

again in Berlin, but the King of Prussia, who had put Howe in prison 11 years before for helping the Poles, still regarded him as a dangerous person, and would not allow him to enter the country. This greatly amused Horace Mann, who wrote to Howe, "I understand the King of Prussia has about 200,000 men constantly under arms, and if necessary he can increase his force to two millions. This shows the estimation in which he holds your single self!"

Mann found the schools in Germany, particularly those in Prussia, the most humanitarian of all in Europe. Most of the credit could be given to Karl Wilhelm von Humboldt, who had been put in charge of a special section of the ministry of the interior in 1807, and had had education put under him. His greatest achievement was the foundation of the University of Berlin. But the one change that so affected Mann was that von Humboldt had, in 1810, introduced a state examination and certification of teachers. This requirement had brought an end to the former common practice of permitting unqualified theological students to teach, and had at once raised the teaching profession to a high level of dignity and efficiency. Von Humboldt had also introduced the teaching methods of Pestalozzi into the teachers' seminaries and had thus vitalized the elementary schools.

In Germany, said Mann, he had yet to see an instance of harshness or severity: "All is kind, encouraging, animating, sympathizing. This last is true to such a degree as would seem almost ludicrous with us. A German teacher evinces the greatest joy at the success of a pupil in answering a question; seems sorrowful, and even deeply moved with grief, if he fails. When a question has been put to a young scholar, which he strove and struggled to answer, I have seen a look

German teachers were overjoyed at a bright reply.

of despair in the teacher; but if the little wrestler with difficulties overcame them, and gave the right answer, the teacher
would seize and shake him ardently by the hand to felici-
tate him upon his triumph; and where the difficulty has been
really formidable, but the exertion on the scholar's part
triumphant, I have seen the teacher seize the pupil in his
arms and embrace him. . . . And all this has been done so
naturally, so unaffectedly, as to excite no other feeling in the
residue of the children than that of a desire to win the same
favor for themselves."

The Manns traveled on to Holland, which Mann noted
was famous for its benevolent institutions.

Mann was curious to see Leyden because it had been for
a time the residence of some of the Pilgrim Fathers. He had
often looked out from the shore of Plymouth, Massachusetts,

"as it were to see them coming, for freedom's sake, to a strange and inhospitable shore." Now he looked out westward from Leyden in his imagination to see them departing on their desolate course. Mann found no memorials to the Pilgrims in Leyden, but did not hold this against the Dutch. The Pilgrims' monuments, he felt, were the free institutions of America, "the career and the capacities of human improvement opened throughout the boundless Western World."

Mann was tired of Europe, and he and Mary would gladly have gone home, but since they were there and might never be able to go again, they went on to Paris. Mann thought that Massachusetts was, on the whole, ahead of almost anything France had to offer. At Versailles, however, he found that the Normal School of France had once been the dog-kennels of Louis XIV and Louis XV, and observed that "a revolution which can turn a dog-kennel into a Normal school has at least one argument in its favor."

At last they felt they could sail for home. April, 1844, found Mann writing to Combe that he wished to heaven an ocean did not separate the two of them. Mann had presented his seventh Annual Report to the Legislature in January, and he knew Combe would want to know about its reception. Generally speaking, Mann thought that the Report had met with unusual favor. But some people had attacked it and him. And some of the attacks were virulent.

"There are owls," wrote Mann, "who, to adapt the world to their own eyes, would keep the sun from rising. Most teachers amongst us have been animated to greater exertions by the account of the best schools abroad. Others are offended at being driven out of the paradise which their own self-esteem had erected for them."

Chapter 11

A Male Child is Born

Mann also reported in his letter to Combe that a son had been born to him and Mary on February 24.

In recognition of that event, Horace Mann started a new diary. His first entry was, "Yesterday at 1/2 past 10 o'clk, P.M. a male child was born to me."

Before the baby's arrival, Sophia Hawthorne had written to her mother, Mrs. Peabody, "I suspect that Mary's baby must open its mouth the moment it is born, and pronounce a School Report: for its mother's brains has had no other permanent idea in it for the last year. It will be a little reincarnation of education systems, a human school."

Horace wrote of his first son, who was also named Horace, "Thinking of him, I am reminded of the beautiful lines from the Arabic, translated by Sir William Jones.

Naked, on parent-knees, a new-born child,
Weeping, thou sat'st, while all around thee smiled.
So live, that sinking to thy last long sleep,
Thou then may'st smile while all round thee weep.

On March 9, Mann wrote, "Tonight, it is just a fortnight since my boy was born. I find my mind more and more interested in him, my feelings more and more alive to his welfare, to his fortunes—his future, unknown fortunes."

For four years, he was to keep a close record of young Horace's development, his health, his character traits. "Whatever may be my own fate or that of the child, I have thought that a record of occurences relating to it, & of my own emotions respecting it, might at some future day be agreeable, & it would enable me to look back upon many things wh. otherwise would sink in oblivion, & would supply an authentic account of facts, instead of fallacious recollections."

The boy was of good size, his father noted, and seemed healthy and well. He also had a look of "at least fair intelligence and capacity." But Mann was concerned lest the little boy might have "too active a temperament from the high nervous temperament of father and mother." This, he thought, would have to be modified by education and training.

Considering his own age, 44, Mann doubted whether he should live to see his first son grow up. "He may be left fatherless as I was, at the age of thirteen, or younger. This is not a consoling prospect. Still more necessary is it, then, that as far as possible he should be conducted into the right path."

Young Horace's most prominent trait, his father thought, was the "exstacies of laughter into which he is [put] by a kind & loving look or smile." Perhaps, Mann pondered, his son was being educated to love company too well. This was his and Mary's fault. Whenever the baby waked, his father and mother went to him, to enjoy themselves in seeing his delight, "a good motive, but an unwise act."

The baby began at one point to show a reluctance to

go to sleep by himself at night. Horace and Mary Mann agreed that they must put him down and leave him alone, in spite of his resistance. "We do not want him to associate the two ideas together of complaining and succeeding."

Mann worried about a "germ of deception" he seemed to discover in his son at two years of age. "For instance, if he wants to open a box & scatter around its contents, he will carry it round behind our chairs, or behind the door, or in some place where he is not seen, for the purpose of doing what he would not attempt to do, if he knew our eyes were upon him. Another is, to ask his mother to go away, when he wishes to do something that he knows would be debarred from doing in her presence. This is a very serious matter. . . ." Here, said Mann, was not only the germ of deception but the laying of a plan to bring off the deception successfully.

The diary was planned as a record of young Horace's progress, but at one point Horace could not resist noting that Mary lived to bless him beyond all his hopes. "I am sorry to say that the temper of the boy is sometimes irritable or fractious; but his mother's gentleness & patience are inexhaustible. She bears whatever comes & uses the softest words to smooth down his excitement. Such a store-house of love as is laid up in her heart is to me a daily marvel."

January 27, 1846, found Mann entering the fact that "One month ago . . . at about 1/2 past 1 o'clk. in the morning, my dear wife produced a second son. . . . What may he be! What will he be! There is not one chance in a hundred that I shall live till he arrives at years of discretion! There is not one chance in a thousand that I shall live till he arrives at years of majority! Oh, how great, how feeble, may be my power over him. Yet such power as I have shall be religiously exercised for his steps along the perilous paths of early life."

Mann concluded that he would not make any more entries respecting his second son, who was named for George Combe. Instead, he bought a journal for Mary to use in recording Georgie's developments from time to time. They would thus "preserve an enduring record of what would otherwise be fleeting, & when once gone, irrecoverable."

Mann made his final entry in the diary devoted to the development of his first son on February 25, 1848: "This is Horace's birth-day. He is four years old. I think a great change has taken place in him within the last year. His health is very good. He is yet a little troubled with the humor that sowed thorns over so much of his early life. He is becoming more manageable or tractable; tho' not yet without turns of disobedience to his mother, but he generally obeys me promptly. Altho' I have never struck him a blow, yet he understands that he must obey me. His disposition is softening. He is full of affection, loves benevolent stories, & the idea of doing good. He is rather too self-conscious; & the love of approbation is a very strong motive in his mind. I think we may have fostered this a little too much; instead of adhering very strictly to the general purpose of doing right because it is right. Of course, I would not exclude this idea of approbation in training, but it is to be managed with great discretion. He has learnt considerably. Can read some short words, & knows at sight the nine digits. He has also a good faculty for drawing, & will make a dog quite like a dog. Care, perseverance, wisdom, I trust, will make a useful & happy man, of what might with his original temperament, have been far otherwise."

A third Mann son, Benjamin Pickman Mann, was born April 20, 1848, and named for Colonel Benjamin Pickman, Mary's childhood idol.

The lives of all three of the Mann children were filled with "honor, virtue, and usefulness," and Mann could have rejoiced in all of them. Benjamin Mann became a botanist, and engaged in philanthropic work. He left part of his estate to the American Association for the Advancement of Science to study the causes of poverty in Massachusetts, and another part to the Massachusetts Historical Society to care for the works of Horace Mann and Elizabeth Peabody.

George Combe Mann was a teacher and became principal of the Jamaica Plain High School. Young Horace also became a botanist. He traveled in Minnesota with Thoreau in 1861. He spent a year in Hawaii, and compiled an outline of Hawaiian plants. He became a tutor in botany at Harvard and acting director of the Harvard Botanic Gardens and Herbarium.

Mary Mann wrote about her boys with love and understanding. After their father died at Antioch College in 1859, two lines which she wrote to a friend tell something of the relationship between the boys and their mother: "My children saved me. George, a little boy then, clung to my side and never left me till one day I remember his saying, 'There, she has smiled!' "

On February 25, 1844, Mann wrote, "Yesterday . . . a male child was born to me."

Twelve years before, when Charlotte died, life itself had seemed to be ended for him. Now, here he had produced life. The solemnity with which he thought about the event at no time obscured the fact that, for him, it was a miracle.

Chapter 12

Paradise was not Destroyed

W hen Mann wrote to George Combe in April of 1844, he also said that some of the attacks made upon him after his seventh Annual Report was published were virulent. He did not make clear—perhaps had not yet fully realized—that he was engaged in a battle that was probably the most virulent in all of this country's educational history.

It has been said that the seventh Report was not so much an important contribution to pedagogical science as it was an important contribution to pedagogical dynamics. It brought on controversy with the Boston schoolmasters that placed Mann's name and beliefs before the public as nothing else could have done.

Mann devoted most of the 178 pages of the seventh Report to his European tour. Mann looked at education broadly in this report, and tried not to draw comparisons between the best of the schools which he had visited abroad and those of Massachusetts. But the schoolmasters did make the comparisons, and found them odious. Particularly the schoolmasters of Boston, who had been generally considered the best of the land, found them so. Up to this time they

had been able to ignore Mann's reforms, and had complacent-
ly gone along in the same old way. While other Massachusetts
teachers were working to improve their methods, learn new
ways of doing things, and bring about better schools, the
masters of Boston did nothing. Mann's report was a mirror.
The Boston people who cared about education looked into
it, and did not much like what they saw. For the first time,
the Boston masters were being scrutinized with something
less than respect.

From the beginning, they had resented Mann, partly
because he was not a professional educator, partly because
he had no respect for methods of teaching just because those
methods had been followed for a hundred years. The Boston
schoolmasters felt that their cup of endurance with Mann
was not only full but running over.

Thirty-one of them got together and wrote and had
published a pamphlet of 141 pages, *Remarks on the Seventh
Annual Report*. It was a personal attack on Mann. They said
again and again, as they had said before, that he was not an
educator. But this time they said it in print. They said he
knew nothing about education. They asked what the Secretary of the Board knew about the Boston schools. "With one
voice," they answered themselves, "he knows comparatively
nothing."

The *Remarks* had four divisions. The last three divisions were less shrill and vindicative than the first, but the
writers of all were implacably opposed to Horace Mann.
They threw back in his face everything good he had written
about the schools of Prussia, the methods he proposed for
remedying the way children were taught to read, his beliefs
that children could be taught without corporal punishment.

"All school order, like that of the family and society," said the fourth division, "must be established upon the basis of acknowledged authority, as a starting point; it is not merely the teacher's right, but his duty as well, to establish and enforce such authority."

One of the final straws came in the controversy when Mann was asked by one of the masters where he had got the $900 he had given "in a big gesture" to the normal schools. Mann's patience was strained, but he did manage to reply quietly enough. "It wasn't without a struggle," he said, "but I sold my law books to get that nine hundred dollars for the Normal School."

Mann invited the Boston schoolmasters to meet him on the public platform. The invitation was not accepted. Instead, a *Rejoinder* to Mann's *Reply,* again consisting of four parts, was issued.

Horace Mann's friends were not idle. Thirty-four of his friends got together to set down their gratitude to him for his devoted efforts on behalf of the common schools.

Charles Sumner prepared the formal draft. It said, in part:

". . . By the mass of your labors you have contributed essentially to the happiness and prosperity of the Commonwealth, and to its fame abroad. Your name helps to make the name of Massachusetts respectable throughout our own country and in distant lands. If then it be true, as has been said, that he is a benefactor who makes two blades of grass grow where only one grew before, how much more is he a benefactor, who infuses new energies into a whole people, doubling in ten thousand souls the capacities for usefulness and happiness. To you as the author of so much good, we wish to offer our sincere thanks. We feel a debt of gratitude, which it will always be a pleasure, still paying, still to owe. These are not mere words, but the spontaneous tribute of the heart. . . ."

Among the signers were Josiah Quincy, Hillard, Loring, Howe, Longfellow, and, of course, Sumner.

Sumner also wrote to the Legislature asking for $5,000 for permanent Normal School buildings at Bridgewater and Westfield, promising to match the amount with private subscriptions. The money was granted.

Mann wrote to Sumner, "If . . . I have ever had any good fortune, or exercised any good judgment in my public life, it was in connecting myself with a cause, which, from its intrinsic merits, was sure to win the regard and favor of all good men."

The battle was not yet ended. Mann had to write his *Answer* to the *Rejoinder*. The pages of the four pamphlets still smoke with charges of falsehood, misrepresentation, and ignorance; but the last two of the pamphlets were calmer in tone than the first two. So far as the principals in the controversy were concerned, the controversy was ended. The Boston schoolmasters and the people concerned with the schools of Boston began to turn their attention to the improvement of those schools.

The battle for the schools went on. It died down in one quarter only to spring up in another. The most orthodox of the ministers came into the fray, some because they honestly believed Mann was trying to keep the children of Massachusetts from believing in God, some because they wanted the publicity.

One of the latter was the Reverend Mathew Hale

Smith, who preached a sermon attacking the Board of Education and its Secretary before the Church and the Society of the Pilgrims in Boston, on October 10, 1846. The preacher gave his sermon the title, "The Ark of God on a New Cart."

Society, charged Smith, had been stricken with immorality and depravity because it, like Uzzah, had neglected the divine commandments. "Modern reformers have taken the education of youth under their special care. . . . Throwing themselves across the word of God, they ridicule as well as forbid the use of the rod." He made it clear that he held the Board of Education responsible for putting the Ark of God on a new cart, and that Horace Mann had profaned the Ark, as Uzzah had done.

The sermon was sensational in its contents and it effects. Smith had to say it all over again to an even larger audience.

"A child of sin and Satan came out in a fierce . . . attack upon the Board . . . and myself," Mann said. No child of Satan would stand in the way of truth.

Mann's public statements at the time do much to define his attitudes toward religion, and his private letters to George Combe do much to tell what he felt about this particular controversy. Throughout it Mann held consistently to his often expressed belief: the Bible should be read aloud in the public schools, but without note or comment. He was firmly opposed to each district's determining the kind of doctrine to be taught in that district ". . . the experiment would not stop with having a dozen conflicting creeds taught by authority of law in the different schools of the same town or vicinity. Majorities will change in the same place. One sect may have the ascendency today, another tomorrow. This year there will be three Persons in the Godhead; next year but one; and the third year the Trinity will be restored to hold its precarious sovereignty until it shall be again dethroned by the worms of the dust it has made. . . ."

To Combe he wrote that the religious fires had been fanned by fanatics who thought it necessary first to put him down that they might afterwards introduce their own religious doctrine into the schools. "The Orthodox are hunting me as though they were bloodhounds, and I a poor rabbit."

Again, Mann's friends rallied to his defence, and again he won the case for his client, the next generation. A particular creed or doctrine would not be pushed upon the children of the Massachusetts schools.

In the midst of all this tumult, Worthy Putnam, who had the supervision of 20,000 youth in Chautauqua County, New York, invited Mann to come speak to them. Mann was sorry not to be able to do it. Then Putnam asked Mann to send an encouraging communication to teachers and pupils.

On July, 1846, Mann sat down to write the letter. It is a memorable one, and was written at a time he was very tired. He had worked 15 to 16 hours a day, every day, from the time he had taken the job as Secretary to the Board of Education in 1837. He had been poorly paid. He had been abused and battered. If there was ever a time when it would have seemed that his faith in education should have wavered, it was now. Instead, this letter, which he wrote from his heart, reflects once again his love of education, and his passionate belief in the eternal educability of man.

He wrote, in part:

". . . The human heart is not like a box, or a trunk, or a bag, which will hold just so much and no more. A boy's heart is not like his vest or his jacket, which would be very small, so small as only to embrace one's self in its thoughts and desires; this makes a very mean, selfish person. The heart may be enlarged so as to embrace a town; this makes a good townsman. Or it may take in one's whole nation; this makes a patriot. Or it may take in all mankind; this makes a philanthropist. Or it may embrace in its affections the whole universe and the great creator of it; this makes one godlike; and, all the way, let me tell you, from the narrowest limit to the vastest expansion, its happiness will be in proportion to its enlargement.

"My young friends I wish to improve this opportunity to impress upon your minds one idea; and as ideas are not so plenty as blackberries, when you can get one that is sound and true, you will do well to keep it, and to think of it a great deal. . . ."

He wrote about many of the things they were not born to do: ". . . You were not made to lie, or to steal, or to use profane or obscene language, or to be intemperate, or to quarrel with your schoolmates, or to be unkind to brothers or sisters, or disobedient to parents and teachers, or to scoff or to mock at what is holy and good. It would be better that you should be flung into the hottest furnace that was ever kindled, than that you should train your tongues to falsehood, and perjury, and blasphemy. . . ."

"Having told you of some things you were not made to do, let me now tell you of some which you were made to do, just as much as the sun was made to radiate light, and not darkness; just as much as the trees were made to grow upwards, and not downwards; just as much as the birds were made to live in the air, and the fishes in the sea, without ever exchanging abodes.

"You were made to be industrious. All your bones and muscles were made for work, just as much as the wheels of a clock or a watch were made to go round; and if you do not work in some way, you are as worthless as the clock *made not to go.* Industry gives health. . . .

"You were made to be temperate. The man who is always temperate enjoys a great deal more, in the long run, than one who gives way to excesses. . . .

"You were made to be clean and neat in your person and in your dress, and gentlemanly and ladylike in your manners. If you have not been bitten by a mad dog, don't be afraid of fresh water. . . .

"You were made to be kind, and generous, and magnanimous. If there is a boy in the school who has a club foot, don't let him know that you ever saw it. If there is a poor boy with ragged clothes, don't talk about rags when he is in hearing. If there is a lame boy, assign him some part of the game which does not require running. If there is a hungry one, give him a part of your dinner. If there is a dull one, help him get his lessons. If there is a bright one, be not envious of him; for if one boy is proud of his talents, and another is envious of them, there are two great wrongs, and no more talents than before. . . .

"Finally, you were made to be moral and religious. Morality consists primarily in the performance of our duties to our fellow-men; religion in the performance of our duties to God. On the sublime and beautiful subject of morality, I have time only to touch upon one thing. That shall be *Honesty.* If all men were honest, we should need no jails or prisons; no bolts nor locks; no high enclosures to keep out garden thieves; no criminal laws or courts. It is a shame to

all mankind that such things are necessary. It seems to me that I should pine and die of mortification, if I thought such things were made for me. I want all of you to feel that such things were not made for you. . . .

"*You must be religious;* that is, you must be grateful to God, obey his laws, love and imitate his infinite excellence. The works of God are full of wonders and beauties. He has laid the foundations of the universe in miracles, and filled it with starry splendors. . . .

"These things, my dear children, and such as these, you were made for. You were made for them, as the rich corn and the delicious fruits were made to grow in the fertile valleys; and may your own efforts, encouraged and aided by divine goodness, enable you to fulfil the purposes of your creation. Remember, though man sinned, Paradise was not destroyed. The sinner was driven from Eden, but Eden itself remained. It can be entered again. You can enter it and make it your own."

Chapter *13*

The Bravest Act

O n Christmas Eve, 1846, Mary and Horace Mann, young Horace and George, moved into their new home in West Newton that Horace had had built for them. It was a fine home on a hill with wide verandas and extensive grounds where Mary and Horace could garden and plant fruit trees and where the boys could play.

"Our life, hitherto," Mary wrote to Sophia Hawthorne, "has been like that steamboat voyage—a toss here & a toss there, & my poor husband bearing the inconveniences like a saint—never having a really comfortable moment to himself. . . ."

Mann echoed Mary when, writing a year later to an old friend, he said, "I have been a wanderer for twenty years and when asked where I lived I answered: 'I do not live anywhere, I board.'"

They were 10 miles from Boston and, naturally enough, only 100 rods from the West Newton Women's Normal School, which Cyrus Peirce directed.

The Manns were hospitable. Members of the Mann household at times included Miss Elizabeth Peabody, Miss

Catherine Beecher, and Rebecca Pennell. Nathaniel T. Allen, principal of the model school, lived with them for a while, as did Mrs. George Walton, who was assistant to Cyrus Peirce, and William B. Fowle, also a distinguished educator. Friends were on all sides of them. Nathaniel Allen had a house on Webster Street. With William Parker and Nathaniel Allen, Horace Mann had a part in establishing the Unitarian Church in West Newton.

The Reverend Samuel F. Smith, who wrote "America," lived in nearby Newton Center, and another of Mann's and Howe's close friends, the Reverend Theodore Parker, lived for a time in nearby Auburndale. One of the happiest times of their lives was the period when Horace and Mary Mann and the children were together there in West Newton.

Mann had never had the ability to accept recreation either for its own sake or for his health's sake. "He had not the art of lying fallow," said Mary, "and thus gathering new strength for labor. His love of children was the only natural outlet for his native hilarity; and this blessed resource was all that saved him when the outside world seemed bent upon harassing him."

He could not turn his sons or other children away when they came to him. "Others had to defend him from their loving inroads," Mary reported, "hunt them in his study, and pick them off his writing desk, and out of the back of his chair, where they would be found perched. No play was so charming as that in which he partook. . . . It came to be necessary to make a rule about taking turns upon his knee; and they learned to watch for the occasions when he laid down his pen, or was alone in the often-sought study, to which all the schoolmasters and school-committee men, educators and would-be educators, earnest inquirers or malcontents, had free access. . . ."

One of the most distinguished of all the educators who visited the Manns at West Newton was Domingo Faustino Sarmiento. What Horace Mann's influence was on the public schools of the United States, Sarmiento's was on the South and Central American schools.

Born in Argentina in 1811, Sarmiento had had to take refuge in Chile at an early age because of his political opinions. He returned to Argentina in 1836, but was imprisoned for writing propaganda against the dictatorship. He managed to escape three years later, again to Chile. There he founded the first Chilean normal school, and was a member of the faculty, at the same time carrying on political and journalistic activities in behalf of liberal government policies and popular education. In 1845, with the help of an eminent Chilean, he was given a commission to study primary education in foreign countries, much as Horace Mann had done. Sarmiento's investigations took him to Spain, Africa, Italy, France, Switzerland and England. His funds were almost gone when he decided he must go on to the United States to find out more about the development of the common schools and the normal schools, and to get to know Horace Mann.

Mann was captivated by Sarmiento's enthusiasm for popular education. For two days the men sat and talked together about every aspect of education in Massachusetts. They visited the normal school in West Newton together. When Sarmiento left, he took with him letters of introduction from Mann to Emerson, Longfellow, and a number of prominent government officials.

[*144*]

Sarmiento lived to be 77 and ultimately was elected president of the Argentine Republic. During his distinguished career, he held many high offices, but the title that he valued most was that of Teacher.

Eighteen years after Sarmiento's visit to Horace Mann in West Newton, the visitor was to say, "I have done nothing but to follow in his steps, taking as a model his great labors. . . . My safest guide, I found it, in the digest of laws and ordinances regulating that beautiful system of schools."

Today in Buenos Aires, a primary school bears the name of Horace Mann. A grade school is named Estados Unidos de America. Several normal schools are named for the pioneer American teachers who helped train young men and women of Argentina to become teachers.

Those happy days in West Newton, when they were all together, were not to last long enough to satisfy either Horace or Mary Mann, or the boys.

On March 15, 1848, Horace Mann was nominated by the Whigs as a candidate for representative of the Eighth District of Massachusetts in Congress. That same day he also received the nomination of the Free Soilers. The Democrats nominated E. K. Whitaker.

All these things occurred because on February 23, John Quincy Adams had died after suffering a stroke on the floor of the House of Representatives two days before. He had represented the people of the Eighth District for 18 years. John Quincy Adams, one of the ablest men ever to serve his state and nation, was so far above human vanity he had been able—after being minister to England, Secretary of State, and President of the United States—to simply and greatly go to the House of Representatives in 1830. To the suggestion that it would degrade a former President to serve in the lower house, he had replied that it degraded no man to serve his fellow citizens as a representative in Congress.

The people of the Eighth District mourned John Quincy Adams, but they did not intend to leave his seat in Congress vacant a minute longer than it would take them to elect a successor. At a time when the entire country was in a state of political ferment over slavery, Massachusetts was recognized as the storm center in the fight for human freedom. The Eighth District was the storm center of Massachusetts. "Turbulent Dedham," which Mann had served in the Legislature, was in that district. The people of the Eighth District had to have their voices heard in Washington. John Quincy Adams had taught them that.

The *Boston Journal* on March 16 congratulated the Whigs on their choice of Horace Mann, and "confidently anticipated" his election: ". . . the good people of the Eighth District will require no pledges from Mr. Mann; they will seek for no exposition of his views on any of the great political questions of the day. They have a guaranty in his past life, that if elected to Congress, he will always be found on the side of reason, justice, and patriotism. . . ."

At first Mann declined the nomination. "To ask anybody in this district to fill Mr. Adams' place," he had written to a friend before the nomination, "is a good deal like asking a mouse to fill an elephant's hide." But it was not fear of being unable to do a good job in Washington, nor was it false modesty, that made Mann decline the nomination at the beginning. He had been too long without a settled home to want to give up the happiness of his life in West Newton with Mary and the boys, as well as his friends.

He expressed some of his doubts to Charles Sumner.

Sumner replied that he would be sorry to see Mann go to Washington unwillingly, his heart elsewhere. But, said Sumner, if Mann did accept, he should write a letter extolling duty above party expediency. "Write a triumphant letter. No man can do so much by a letter as yourself. You can show, as no other man can, how supreme is duty, above all the suggestion of 'expediency,' and the urgency of party dictation. You can vindicate the importance of the individual. Avowing a hatred of slavery, you can well renounce the slavery of party. Such a letter will strengthen all Massachusetts."

Finally, Mann decided to accept the nomination. One reason for so doing he explained in a letter to Combe. It was, he wrote, a time of crisis "when the destiny of our new Territory of about six hundred thousand square miles . . ." was to be determined. "All of human history . . . and my own twelve years' struggle to imbue the public mind with an understanding . . . of the spirit of religious liberty, had so magnified my horror of all forms of slavery, that even the importance of education itself seemed for the moment to be eclipsed." Also, he said, his health was greatly suffering, and Mary and his friends felt that the time in Washington might give him some rest from the arduous duties as Secretary. Moreover, although he did not tell Combe, his financial need was great. Finally, and perhaps the deciding consideration, he thought that from Washington he might be able to accomplish as much for education within the nation as he had accomplished in Massachusetts. He sat down and wrote his acceptance. He said, "A state of true and universal education would imply the highest state of earthly existence, but freedom is the prerequisite of education."

Horace Mann was elected to Congress by a majority of 1,350. His support came principally from those who believed that he was opposed to slavery.

Mann wrote to Combe: "On the 13th of April I went to Washington. Soon after, I resigned my Secretaryship; but the Board, not being prepared to appoint a successor, requested me to continue to discharge its duties till the close of the year. This I consented to do, especially as it would afford me an opportunity to make a final report. . . . Thus, instead of being a relay, I was made to run double stages—to perform the duties of a member of Congress, and by correspondence to carry on the Secretaryship."

Horace Mann took rooms near the Capitol. Once again he was not living anywhere, just boarding. To Cyrus Peirce he wrote, "I find myself as comfortably situated here as I could expect; but I have not the slightest expectation of ever feeling any attachment for the position. . . . I have seen enough already to give me even a deeper conviction of the necessity and indispensableness of education than I ever had before. It is the only name whereby a republic can be saved."

He reported on his activities to Mary: "I take one or two walks every day in the grounds at the east of the Capitol —such green grass, such beautiful flowers. I can send you a few flowers. I wish I could send you half an hour of birds' singing." Mary could hardly conceive how beautiful Washington was, he said.

He was worried about the arrival of the expected baby, and he urged Mary to take care of her health. Benjy arrived safely at 6:00 P.M. on April 30. "This is the quietest, most

[148]

comfortable baby we have ever had, he only sleeps & eats," Mary wrote her husband.

One of the older boys, Mary later recorded, had planted himself upon the hall stairs after his father's departure for Washington, "every day, for a month, to 'wait for papa,' and could hardly be torn from his post." For them "to be 'little papas' to the new-born babe was the most grateful form of consolation."

Although Mann needed the money and wanted to write the twelfth Annual Report, it was probably mistaken judgment on his part to retain the Secretaryship of the Board of Education until a successor could be found. That did not happen until December 1, 1848, after Mann had been re-elected to Congress in November. During his first month in Congress, he was continually plagued by the countless duties and very considerable correspondence that had to be carried on by him as Secretary. He did not get the rest Mary and his friends had wanted for him. Nor did he have the time to give full attention to his duties as Congressman.

Also, so long as he remained Secretary to the Board of Education, he thought that he must remain neutral in the expression of his opinions on many of the important issues involving slavery. Sumner, and even Howe, became increasingly impatient. "*Yours* is the voice of power," Sumner wrote Mann at one point. "What you say must produce an echo. I desire that it shall commence its work of influence soon."

Mann said in one of his answers to Sumner's many letters: "You may depend upon it, you are mistaken in your opinion that I am tardy about speaking. Such an attempt would be looked upon as rash, even by those here who think as I do on the general subject. No occasion has yet arisen that would furnish me with a fair opportunity. The territory question is the question. That will be up ere long. Then I may try. But as yet, it is premature." Mann said on another occasion that Sumner and Howe seemed to forget that he was still Secretary of the Board of Education.

Sumner would have none of Mann's reasons. "I perceive that you will be called upon to make sacrifices and to give offense," he wrote. "You counted upon that doubtless when you consented to go to Congress. But I would have you back at the head of our schools, unless you feel able and willing to be the champion of Freedom, as you have already been the champion of Education. . . ."

In April of 1848, Mann described in a letter to Mary the beginning of what was to become one of the most celebrated trials of the day, and one in which he was to be deeply involved. Captain Daniel Drayton had chartered a small coasting vessel, the *Pearl*, owned by Captain Sayres, and had gone to Washington to help a number of slaves escape to Philadelphia. The two captains, a one-man crew, and 74 Negroes, many of them already freed, were aboard the *Pearl* when it was overhauled by a small steamboat carrying 35 armed men. Drayton, Sayres, and the Negroes were brought back to Washington and put in jail. The crew man escaped but was later captured.

Joshua Reed Giddings, member of Congress from Ohio, rushed to the jail as soon as he heard of the arrest and assured the prisoners that they would have legal counsel and support. After visiting Drayton and Sayres, he rose on the floor of the House of Representatives to move an inquiry as to why 76 people were in jail in the District of Columbia "for attempting to vindicate their inalienable rights."

Feeling was very intense in the North about the Drayton affair. In Boston, public meeting was held in Faneuil Hall, and a large committee was appointed to raise funds and employ counsel to defend Drayton and Sayres. Sumner and Howe immediately began to put great pressure on Mann to take the case.

Mann wrote to Howe on May 1 that he was not afraid to take the case, and had even decided to offer his help before Howe's letter came. But, said Mann, he had long been out of court, and was oblivious of the rules of evidence. "I should probably be about the worst counsel the poor fellows could have." He would take the case anyhow, however, because no other lawyer in Washington was willing to defend them. Nothing but a miracle, as Mann saw it, could save them.

One Washington lawyer, J. M. Carlisle, agreed to assist Mann. Carlisle was retained because of his knowledge of Maryland law, which was in force in the District of Columbia. "I am told by Mr. Hall," Mann wrote Howe, "that Judge Crawford, who is to try this case, had decided some time ago, that to take a slave from his master, *in order to set him free,* is stealing."

He wrote Howe again: "The indictments are found by the grand jury. How many do you think there are? There were seventy-four slaves, and forty-one different owners of them. There are forty-one different indictments against each prisoner, [the two captains and the crew man] for stealing *the* slaves of each owner—41 times 3 equals 123; and 74 indictments against each prisoner for enticing away, etc., each slave—74 times 3 equals 222, and 123 plus 222 equals 345 indictments. The secret of this is that the district attorney here is paid $10 each, for every indictment found by the grand jury." Slavery had many kinds of profits.

Still Sumner nagged at Mann. He wanted more aggressiveness on Mann's part. He urged more action. Finally, Mann's patience reached an end: On June 24, he wrote: "My dear Sumner:

"I think you are rather the hardest taskmaster since Pharoah; and I am not quite sure that I ought to stop with that old Egyptian scamp.

"You know I am not only acting-Secretary of the Massachusetts Board of Education, and now keeper of a sort of intelligence office on certain subjects for the whole country, (in which capacity I have literally had thirty letters to open and answer in a day since I have been here) but you also know that I came into the class here when the other members of it had read the book half through; so that I had the back lessons all to make up. You also wanted me to undertake the defense of the 'Pearl' prisoners, who will be arraigned next week. . . . You have been drumming me up for a speech and now you want me to go to Worcester. Is not all this a little too bad?"

Mann was already well into his preparation for a speech, but he did not tell Sumner this. Earlier, however, Mann had written Mary of his plans. He told her that he was laying out the "foundations of a speech on the grounds of admitting new territory to the Union. This is the great question. All Oregon is now to be provided with a new territorial government & if we obtain New Mexico & Upper California, provision must be made for them. Shall they be permitted to hold slaves in those territories or shall they not? This is the greatest question of the age. Several speeches have already been delivered on it in the House & it is now under regular debate in the Senate. I mean to prepare myself as well as I can."

On June 30 Mann delivered his speech. To Mary he wrote that he thought he had made out poorly. But the correspondent of the *Baltimore Patriot,* who was not overly sympathetic with Mann's position, reported that as soon as Mann obtained the floor, the House became "all attention. He commenced speaking, and it was found that fame had not done him injustice." His speech, said the correspondent, was "rich in illustration, forcible in argument, easy and unaffected in style, which, by those who listened to it will not soon be forgotten. It was, by far, the best, the most forcible, and convincing speech, that has yet been delivered on the side of the vexed question. Horace Mann has done himself and his State honor this day. . . ."

Sumner wrote, ". . . You now have a vantage ground which I pray you use for the cause of Freedom. . . ."

The Drayton-Sayres trial began on July 27. Washington was not only hot with the white heat of controversy; the weather itself was "Tophet," wrote Mann to Howe. Slaveholders and sympathizers with the slavery cause appeared in court with "cocked pistols and dirks."

Mary Mann urged her husband not to risk his life needlessly to the fury of people who believed in slavery. He reassured her. The South would not risk giving the North a martyr at this time. But to Theodore Parker, he wrote that the courtroom during the first days of the trial was "packed like a slave-ship," and that within springing distance of him was a man who "drew his pistol on Drayton." Mann wrote his wife the day after the trials opened that things looked

[*153*]

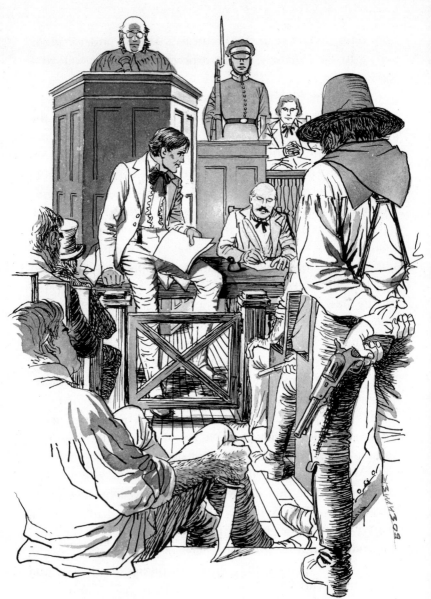

Tempers ran high in the sweltering courtroom.

"pretty squally." Horace Mann had a fight on his hands.

The U. S. District Attorney for the District of Columbia was Philip Barton Key, son of Francis Scott Key and a relative of Chief Justice Taney. Key attempted to invoke a Maryland act of 1737 that carried the death penalty for stealing slaves.

Mann argued the case, with what he considered excellent help from Carlisle, for 21 days. His letters to Mary reflect his moods and appraisals of the situation as it progressed:

August 5: "We had a verdict of 'guilty' returned yesterday against Drayton. The jury were in consultation twentyone hours. We understand that those who stood out for the prisoner were at last induced to surrender by the fear of losing all patronage and custom in the city if they refused to convict. . . ."

August 7: "Notwithstanding we have reverses, yet I think the law is on our side; and we mean so far to get the principles on record, that, if we fail here, we can get the decision reversed in a higher court. . . . I am told that public opinion in this District is undergoing a change."

August 10: "Ah! The verdict was against us again yesterday. It seems impossible here, at the present time, to have an impartial trial. No jury, in a free State, would have convicted Drayton in either of the cases. . . . We must struggle hard yet. They have not yet got him hopelessly in their clutches."

At last, the crew man was acquitted and Drayton and Sayres were saved from the penitentiary. Each was fined $10,-000, however, and held in jail until their fines should be paid. Since neither had the money, and the Abolitionists could not raise it, they remained imprisoned until they were pardoned by President Fillmore on August 11, 1852. Their imprisonment had lasted four years and nearly four months.

Before the appellate court, Mann said, "If man is charged with stealing an animal, free by nature, the prosecutor must prove that he has tamed the animal, or in some other way reduced it to possession. But under the ruling of Judge Crawford in the Court below, although the number of free colored people in the District who are as incapable of being reduced to slavery as the whites themselves, now preponderates over the number of slaves, probably in the proportion of three to one, yet Judge Crawford's law makes every colored person *prima facie* a slave."

Mann illustrated his argument by saying that if foxes in England could escape the noblemen's parks and recover their natural liberty, they would no longer be subject to theft, for no one would have ownership in them. But, by Judge Crawford's law, he said, Negroes were treated worse than foxes under English common law.

While Mann was speaking, Key, the U. S. attorney, wrote the following on a small piece of paper, and laid it on Mann's table just as he finished his argument:

> *To illustrate the point he's making,*
> *In larceny there must be 'taking,'*
> *A fox, he says, cannot be stolen,*
> *Be he young, or be he an old 'un.*
> *Pursuing hound, says he's mistaken,*
> *At least so far as to th' 'Taking.'*

Mann, with his thought of the $10 Key was receiving for each indictment, wrote on the back of the paper:

> *Fox-hunting abroad, and slave-hunting indoors,*
> *I beg leave to suggest, do not run on all fours.*

Foxes do not catch foxes; brute natures have bounds,
But Mr. District Attorney, outhounding the hounds,
Hunts men, women and children—his pockets to fill—
On three hundred indictments, at Ten Dollars a Bill.

In September of 1848, the Whigs unanimously renominated Mann at their convention in Dedham, and the Free Soil convention at Dorchester later in the month also renominated him unanimously. He was reelected on November 7, 1848, receiving 11,000 of the 13,000 votes cast.

During the years he was in Congress, Horace Mann wrote Mary almost daily letters, reporting on life in Washington. Although such major issues as the tariff, internal improvements, and the U. S. Bank were before the House and the Senate, his personal convictions and interests led him to follow almost exclusively, and report to Mary, the developments of the slavery issue and the new territories.

He wrote to the boys, too, little notes that young Horace could read aloud to George. When Horace was four, one of his father's notes to him asked, "Cannot Horace write Papa a letter, alone, and without Mama's helping him?" A little later he was asking whether Horace talked French with Mama a little every day.

He told them about the boy pages in the House. He wrote: "When the Clerk has read all about what was done the day before, then a great many gentlemen spring up and say Mister Speaker, Mr. Speaker, Mr. Speaker, because they all have something they want to say. Sometimes the gentlemen want paper, then one of the boys runs and brings some, oh how quick, they run."

In August of 1849, Mann received a pleasant surprise.

[*157*]

His old friend from Mrs. Clarke's boardinghouse, Dr. Jared Sparks, wrote him. Sparks was now President of Harvard, and Mann had been given the honorary degree of Doctor of both Natural and Civil Laws.

In the spring of 1850, Daniel Webster, senator from Massachusetts, made what became known as his "Seventh of March" speech. "I wish to speak today," he said, "not as a Massachusetts man, not as a Northern man, but as an American. . . . I speak for the preservation of the Union. . . ."

In the preceding January, Henry Clay, senator from Kentucky, had introduced his compromise resolutions providing that California should be admitted as a free state; that territorial governments should be established in the remainder of the Mexican cession without any action by Congress with respect to slavery, letting each territory decide for itself; that slave trade should be abolished in the District of Columbia; and that Congress should enact a more drastic fugitive slave law.

In the great debate which followed, John C. Calhoun, senator from South Carolina, had spoken against the compromise. Now Webster spoke for it.

Mann wrote Mary the following day: "Mr. Webster spoke yesterday; and (can you believe it?) he is a fallen star!—Lucifer descending from heaven! . . . His intellectual life has been one great epic, and now he has given a vile catastrophe to its closing pages. . . . He has walked for years among the gods. . . . I am overwhelmed. . . ."

Mann read Webster's speech carefully. How could Webster atone for the abandonment of the Territories to what he calls "the law of Nature for the exclusion of slavery. . . . The existence or nonexistence of slavery depends more

[158]

upon conscience than climate. . . ."

To Samuel Downer, he wrote that he need say nothing about Webster's support of the enactment of a more drastic fugitive slave law. "While Massachusetts citizens are imprisoned in Southern ports, I think fugitive slaves will be gentlemen at large in Massachusetts."

By April 6, a month later, the intensity of Mann's feelings had not diminished. "Public affairs are looking worse here," he wrote Mary, ". . . more dangerous for the cause of liberty than ever. The defection of Mr. Webster is dreadful. . . . I fear the cause is lost."

Mann decided he must go into the battle against Webster and write to his constituents, which he did in two letters dated May 3 and July 8, 1850, published as pamphlets.

On the day he took his first letter against Mr. Webster to the printer, Mary later recorded, he said, "I am going to do the most reckless thing, on my own account, which I have ever done, in publishing this letter. A thousand of the most prominent men in Massachusetts will never speak to me again. But I must do it; and I shall probably follow it up with more."

To understand what Mann meant, it is important to understand the place Webster had held for years in the minds and hearts of the people of Massachusetts. He was one of the ablest lawyers of the land. He had represented his state nobly in both the U. S. House and the Senate. Massachusetts' mightiest orator, he lifted men above themselves to a nobler world when he spoke. As he walked the streets of Boston, people reached out to touch his coat sleeve as he passed. The dignity of his solid figure, his flashing dark eyes, the music of his voice—all these gave greater splendor to his spoken words than can be recaptured through reading them.

Many historians in later and calmer years would agree that Webster, as well as Henry Clay, was acting to avert civil war, and that their patriotism urged them to put forward their compromise proposals. But Mann spoke for the New England conscience when he opposed Webster; and all the antislavery men of the North agreed with him that Webster's support of the compromise was a bid for Southern votes.

Webster was dumbfounded. He could not believe the bitterness of the reaction to his speech, and he reacted with bitterness to it.

Mann carried forth his fight with great vigor, and it had its effects. Theodore Parker wrote how thankful he was to Mann for writing such a noble letter to Mann's friends and constituents. "God bless you for it!" Parker himself had intended to write, he said, but he was glad he had not done it; for if he had, it might have prevented Mann "from doing better than any one has done hitherto."

Mann's challenge to Webster was, Samuel Hoar said—and he had been for many years an ardent Whig—the bravest act of Mann's life. It was not only proof of Mann's supreme courage, but the "foundation of his political greatness."

It seemed that Webster's political life was ended. But on July 10, 1850, Mann was writing to Mary: "Long before this reaches you, you will have heard that Gen. Taylor [the President] is gone. It is indeed a sad event for the country. . . . He poised himself between the North and the South. . . . With the balance-wheel gone, Mann felt sure that the Southerners would strike again, and there would "not be firmness nor force enough in all the North to resist them."

[*160*]

President Fillmore succeeded Taylor, and appointed Webster his Secretary of State. With that appointment went patronage in Massachusetts. People who had been on his side, Mann wrote Downer, were now as heedless of him, his character, his interests, his feelings, as though he were one of the slaves whom they were "willing should be created. It is saddening, disheartening. I feel it for myself some: I feel it for human nature more."

Webster was the leader of the Whigs, and he decreed that Mann should not get the Whig nomination in October. Even so, Mann lost the nomination by only six votes.

Earlier, however, again in Dedham, Mann was again unanimously nominated by the Free Soilers; and he gave his only speech of that campaign in that town on November 6th. The election in November was a close one: Mann received 6,702 votes; Walley, the Whig candidate, 4,286; and Whitaker, the Democratic candidate, 2,240.

In 1852, Mann was nominated by the Free Soil party for governor of Massachusetts. His whole feeling about the nomination was summed up in a sentence of a letter to Howe: "I have no desire to be in any political office, *per se.*"

In the same letter he said that the Free Will Baptists were erecting buildings for a college at Yellow Springs, Ohio. "They have liberal endowment & aim high. I have been applied to, to navigate that ship. What do you think of it?" Howe thought little of it, and would have no part in encouraging Mann even to think of accepting the offer.

But Mann had learned that the Christian denomination were the sponsors, not the Free Will Baptists as he had thought. The Christians were as liberal in their beliefs, so it seemed, as the Unitarians. The college would be coeducational. There would not have to be required chapel. The West was opening, and this college could be a testing center for the education of the whole United States.

Mann made no campaign for the governorship in 1852. He did not make a single speech or write a single letter to promote his election.

Mann accepted the presidency of the college in Ohio. It was decided to name it Antioch in honor of "the place where men were first called Christian."

Chapter 14

The Towers of Faith

The two most important moves of Horace Mann's professional life—when he assumed the Secretaryship of the Massachusetts Board of Education and when he accepted the Presidency of Antioch College—brought few words of encouragement from his friends. Sumner said bluntly that he should stay home in Massachusetts. Theodore Parker thought Ohio was not worthy of him.

Mary Mann must have had doubts, too, but she kept them to herself. She hated leaving their beloved home, but she consoled herself that at least the family would all be together again. In any case, she did not intend to disagree with anything her husband wanted to do.

Mann himself had no qualms. He wrote to Mary, "I am a free man again. What a Congressional life I have had! But I have fought a good fight, and come out with a clear conscience."

It was not to escape from political life, however, that Mann decided to accept the Antioch presidency. He wanted to get back to education, and he had ideas he wanted to put into effect in a college.

Two of these ideas had been expressed by the delegates of the Christian Church when they had decided at their national convention in October, 1850, to establish the college. This college, they said, "shall afford *equal* privileges to *both sexes.*" In addition, after a great deal of discussion, the delegates had finally decided to accept the recommendation of the Reverend Eli Fay and establish the college without sectarian bias. Mann could hardly believe that a group of religious delegates anywhere in the country could have such a liberal conception of higher education, a conception that agreed so fully with his own beliefs.

Then, too, he wanted to go West again. From his visit to Ohio years before with the Combes, he had a memory of the broad prairies. To him they represented freedom— "freedom," said Mary Mann, "from all that fettered or darkened the human soul through the agency of man."

He accepted the offer to go to Antioch, therefore, not only to the astonishment of his friends, but of the representatives of the Christian denomination as well. They had not dared hope when they approached such an eminent educator, they said, that he would consider their offer seriously. They did not know Horace Mann.

He set about selecting his faculty, and preparing a course of study. First of all, he chose Rebecca Pennell, his niece, to be the first "Professoress." He asked her brother, Calvin Pennell, to join the faculty. Rebecca had been considered the jewel of the Lexington normal school, and Calvin was first in his class at Colby in "sheer intellect."

Surprises were in store for Mann, too. First of all, he discovered that the trustees of the new college, alone, would select the faculty, and that they desired to have the majority belong to the Christian denomination. There was some opposition, too, to the idea of a "professoress," even though the college was to be coeducational. Mann held firm for Rebecca and Calvin Pennell; but he was forced, for the most part, to accept a faculty chosen by others, some as orthodox as any of his orthodox opponents in the days of his Secretaryship. The trustees had ideas about the course of study, also, but Eli Fay wrote Mann that they had held off from imposing them: "We thought it hardly right to take the Mann without his 'Plan.'"

In November of 1852, Mann held his first faculty meeting at his home in West Newton. This time his surprise was a pleasant one. The Reverend Thomas Holmes, Ira Allen, the Pennells, and Mr. Fay were all there, and they remained for about three days. In the course of their discussions about the new college and the courses to be offered, Mann discovered that all were "teetotallers; all anti-tobacco men; all anti-slavery men; a majority of us believed in Phrenology; all anti-emulation men, that is all against any systems of rewards and prizes designed to withdraw the mind from a comparison of itself with a standard of excellence. . . ." They all agreed, too, Mann believed, that there should be a religious atmosphere at Antioch, and chapel exercises, but that attendance at these chapel exercises should not be required.

In December of 1852, Mann was on a lecture tour in Ohio; he spent two days in Yellow Springs making a tour of inspection with Judge William Mills, whose gift of 20 acres of land and several thousand dollars had determined Yellow Springs as the site for Antioch College. Judge Mills, like Mann, had great dreams, and was by nature optimistic.

Together, he and Mann envisioned a college that would be as large or larger than Harvard, with an intellectual climate that would not be surpassed by any college in the country.

The money to build such a college would, of course, be forthcoming. The Reverend Austin Craig, an ardent young Christian minister with a love of learning equal to Mann's, had first interested Mann in Antioch. Craig had assured him that agents who had been soliciting money "have secured $100,000 as a permanent fund for the support of the instructors, together with $30,000 for the erection of buildings." The Christians were not a wealthy sect, but their belief in their college, Mann was convinced, would lead them to see that it was adequately financed.

In June of 1853, Mann wrote Judge Mills to find out what progress was being made in the building of Antioch. Mills assured Mann that everything was in good order.

Mary and Horace Mann, young Horace, Georgie, and Benjy arrived in Yellow Springs in September, 1853. Everything was not in good order, and Judge Mills was not there to reassure Mann. There is no better description of the arrival of the Manns in Yellow Springs than that given by Mary Mann.

"The ambitious brick towers of Antioch College were the first objects to be seen on approaching the spot." They are still the first objects to be seen from several miles away when one approaches Yellow Springs, and Antioch students and alumni, when they see the towers rising, as Mr. Mann said, "aspiringly to the sky," know that they are almost home.

Everything was unfinished. Mr. Mann once tried to describe the state of things, Mary Mann reported, by "saying, that, 'supposing creation had lately issued out of chaos, it might be about as late in the week as Wednesday!'"

The College was "situated on a table-land, which, two years previously, had been despoiled of a magnificent forest to make way for that source of Western wealth, wheat. The stumps of the trees [were] still standing at the very threshold of the college. . . . There was not even any one standing ready to receive the new president, except one of his own relatives [perhaps Calvin Pennell] who had arrived three days before him. No house had been built for his accommodation, as had been promised; nor had he received any intimation of the fact. No provision had even been made for a temporary residence of ten persons; but, happily, a large boarding-house, whose summer residents had left but a few weeks before, was by much persuasion opened to him at the moment. There were not many comforts in it: but he and his friends were strung up to a high tension of nervous energy, having been forewarned, by one who knew something of Western life, that 'the change from the quiet comforts of a New-England home would be found a matter both for laughter and tears'; and the party took possession of the deserted rooms, which they were allowed to arrange for themselves, and which, by dint of a few old stoves, were made habitable for a fall residence. . . ."

The committee in charge of the inauguration of Horace Mann as first president of Antioch College did not dare give out much publicity about the event. The village of Yellow Springs could not accommodate many persons, it was felt, and the chapel might not be finished in time. When October 5, 1853, the day of the inauguration, arrived, however, 3,000 guests arrived with it, all of them come to hear Horace Mann speak. These people of Ohio were accustomed to going many miles in wagons and carriages for revival meetings, corn huskings, or political conventions. They brought their provisions, blankets, and Bibles with them. Many of them cooked over campfires and slept in their wagons or on the ground.

The whole inauguration had a religious fervor about it.

At 10 o'clock on the morning of the 5th, the board of trustees, Mr. Mann, the members of the faculty, and a few honored guests assembled on a platform at the east front of Antioch Hall, the building with the towers. The spectators surged below. After music and prayer, the Reverend John Phillips presented Mr. Mann with three Bibles, "in the name of the Great God, as the constitution of the world." Mann responded in appropriate words, commenting that the Bible "is a book which contains the truths that are able to make men wise unto salvation."

At 12 o'clock, a procession was formed, and moved into the College chapel. Some 1,500 guests also crowded into the room. More prayers were said; Mann was presented with the charter and keys to Antioch College. Eventually, he delivered his inaugural address, which was what people had come to hear. It contained approximately 26,000 words, and covered a wide range of topics—the art of teaching, the needs for both literature and science, the possibilities in human nature, the grace of religion, the responsibilities of educated men and women.

Mann said, "Let us dedicate this college to the two great objects,—which can never be rightfully separated from each other—the honor of God and the service of man: let us renewedly consecrate our own hearts to the worship of our Father in Heaven and to the welfare of our brethren

[*168*]

upon earth." Mann had set his seal on Antioch.

Many people were in tears. After it was all over, Thomas Starr King, a famous Unitarian minister, said that there was enough vitality in that inaugural address "to make the college thrive in Sahara."

When it was all over, boards were laid upon saw horses for the dinner party of the day in the uncompleted dining room. "One hundred and fifty students entered on the afternoon of the inauguration ceremony. The boards were swept, and the examination-papers laid upon them; and these alternate ceremonies of eating and examining went on for two or three days. . . ."

Eight students were found acceptable for admission to Antioch. Most of the others—many of them mature men and women, ministers and teachers among them—entered the preparatory school. Mann knew that there would be many students who would want to enter Antioch, but would not at first meet the high academic standards that he intended to see maintained; and he set up this second school to prepare students for the first. There were a number of Negro students over the years in the preparatory school, and at least eight Negro graduates of Antioch in the years before 1900. The classes contained students of several different religious denominations—Mann mentions Presbyterian and Catholic as well as Christian and Unitarian.

Robert L. Straker has described those early classes: "Of the 327 college and preparatory school students enrolled in 1853-54, 252 were residents of Ohio; the others show a very wide geographical distribution. After the first two years the college enrollment rose sharply, to stabilize around one hundred.

"Several among the first college students were experienced and mature in judgment and character. These more serious and industrious students set a high standard of scholarship and conduct, fulfilling Mann's hopes for a superior college tradition.

"Mann lectured widely in Ohio and neighboring states. Following each of his forays there was a new rush of students —too much raw material all at once—resulting in total registration increasing to more than five hundred. Although only forty students were graduated during Mann's presidency, 325 other college students and more than 1,500 preparatory school students passed under his influence during those six years."

That influence was very great. One of the graduates of the first graduating class of 1857 said that "He stood before his class in the denunciation of slavery and the principles of slave power in the South like the incarnate wrath of the justice of God."

"He watched with great solicitude the movements of those entrusted to his charge," a member of the faculty reported. "Day after day I have known him to consume hours, reasoning, remonstrating, expostulating with students in whom he saw some unfaithfulness of spirit, or some pernicious habit developing itself. . . . He did feel responsible for the health, the purity, the improvement of the young men and women under his charge. He sought the welfare of the students. Nothing gave him more pleasure than to mark improvement in their character."

Part of Horace Mann's influence over the students of Antioch must have sprung from his physical appearance and his manners as much as from his character.

He was just under six feet tall and weighed 190 pounds, but carried himself so erectly that he seemed slender. "His hair was abundant and remarkably white, crowning his unusually high forehead. In repose his clear eyes were mild and friendly; in conflict they were piercing and steadfast as an eagle's. . . . His smile was described as discriminating, not broad and good-humored, as though his affections were to be approached through his reason." Both he and Mrs. Mann dressed with great care, and some elegance. He could be stern. He could be sarcastic. But he had a natural courtesy that all felt who knew him.

There are few reminiscences recorded by Mann's students that are not exalted in tone. He seemed to be "beyond all human weakness" to one of them. He seemed to them "like a prince." Mann, after the trials of Congress, found the Antioch students refreshing, and he gave them his love along with his discipline.

The manners of many of the students were crude. Many of the men, in the manner of the day, smoked raw, native cigars upon their arrival at Antioch, or chewed great quantities of cut plug. Many of them had been accustomed to drinking whiskey. A great number of them had played cards. Mann, in spite of the fact that he had been the best whist player at Litchfield and had drunk rum or wine on occasion, intended to have no drinking, card playing, or smoking at Antioch. He tried to get rid of these habits of students by example, by persuasion, by social pressure; but, if need be, he did it by regulation. He had observed, he said, that men who drank and gambled wasted at least a fourth of their mental vigor, and that, as a legislator, he had found that men who sat long at the card table seldom accomplished

[*171*]

anything but to become card players. Smoking was a dirty habit, and a waste of health and money. Drinking ruined health and happiness, and wasted money. Lying was not only immoral; it was a waste of time.

"So far as I have observed in this life," Mann told his students, "ten men have failed from defect in morals where one has failed from defect in intellect."

President and Mrs. Mann by personal example, respect for others, and general way of life gave these students something most of them had never known before. The whole man, they began to discover, had both a sound body and a developed mind. "Go forth and teach," Mann told them over and over again—the ways of honesty, the ways of intellectual rebirth, the ways of freedom of the body, the mind, and the spirit.

Many of these students, Mary Mann wrote, "found that within themselves which they had not dreamed to exist; and their enthusiasm became equal to the joyfulness of the discovery. It is astonishing how rapidly young people ripen under favorable circumstances; and they carried a new life back to the homes from which they had come."

Mann's personal interests were reflected in the nine women and thirty-one men who were graduated from Antioch while he was president. All of the women were married. Nine of the group became teachers (five of the nine, college professors) ; seven became lawyers (including one Congressman) ; four became ministers (three of them, Unitarians) ; three were physicians; three were businessmen; two were doctors; one was a lecturer; and one was a naturalist. Four of the men died during the Civil War, fighting on the Union side.

At first the Manns ate in the common dining halls, and they continued to do so after they could have stopped because Mann felt that only by their doing so could they introduce certain refinements and manners that he felt important to the students. The Manns had their difficulties. The superintendent of the College was jealous of his powers, and whatever Mann wanted done was almost certainly opposed by the superintendent. The kitchen staff did not have time to prepare and serve meals well, he said. It took almost a battle to get plates changed for dessert. There were stools instead of chairs at the tables; and when some of the women of the faculty bought their own chairs, the superintendent said it was "undemocratic."

Students were encouraged to "get in, eat, and get out," for the convenience of the staff of the commons. The Manns insisted that the students spend at least a half-hour in good conversation at dinner. Soon, the students were looking forward to this period when they talked with each other and the faculty about their philosophies and hopes and fears. Mrs. Clarke would not have enjoyed those conversations, because gossip was discouraged. But how Elizabeth Peabody would have loved them!

When Horace and Mary Mann and the three boys moved into their own home at the edge of the campus, they held at least one levee each term for faculty and students at their beautiful house with great, tall windows, white woodwork, walnut and mahogany furniture, and many books. A large portrait of Dr. Channing hung over the mantle in the library. The doors of the four principal rooms on the first floor folded back to make one large parlor. The faculty dressed with unusual care on these occasions, and came to the levees with white gloves and in their best clothes—meaning that they dressed with care, not luxuriously. The faculty did this in part so that students would learn how they should dress when they were invited out as guests. It was part of the Manns' plan for bringing the influences of civilization to these young people of the West.

No one, however, could do anything about the mud in the rainy seasons of Ohio, which were many. Each person brought an extra pair of shoes when it rained, or carried a scraper to take off the mud. And always when it rained, the light green carpet had to be covered with muslin, which was washed after the levee was over.

Yellow Springs turned out to be twice as turbulent as Dedham ever had been, and much more unrestrained. Mr. Mann, reported Mary, "could not prevent the Ohio pigs from walking through the dining-room [at the College], as there were no fences around the college-buildings, no doors to the hall, and no appointed homes for the animals. Water stood over shoes between the main college-building and the dining-hall . . . so deep that boards floated on it. One day a professor [a lady] was arrested, on her entrance to the hall, by a hog of unusual dimensions, which had made his watery bed where a doorstep should have been. She looked at it in dismay a moment, and then, being light of foot, tripped over it as if it had been a bridge, and sprang over a board which had been inserted where the door should have been hung, the board having been placed there by some friendly hand to prevent the intrusion of *living* bridges." The Ohio students could laugh about the stepping stones in the mud that got up and walked away, but the casual appearance of pigs in the parlor were a trial to the Manns and the teachers who had

Hogs came to dinner with the human beings.

come from somewhat better ordered communities.

Social life was encouraged. Mann remembered his own student days at Brown and Litchfield. Although permission had to be granted by the president or matron for dates, walks, or buggy rides, it was seldom denied. Secret societies of any kind were forbidden, but there were literary societies, musicales, teas, readings, debates, and, at small parties in private homes, dancing was permitted.

Moncure Conway in his *Autobiography* gave a brief

account of life at Antioch under Mann. Conway was a famous Unitarian minister, who brought a number of his freed slaves (he called them "house servants," even though he was a Virginian originally) to Yellow Springs and settled them in the community. Once when he was visiting Yellow Springs, staying at the local inn, he said, "The glen near by and the warm morning invited me to a stroll beside the clear brook which flows with frequent cascades through a mile of green banks and wild flowers. Suddenly I came upon a troop of young ladies, each carrying a book and a botanical box. One of them . . . I had met; she introduced me to the professor —a handsome lady, who invited me to participate in their exercises. The glen was their recitation-room in spring for botany and geology.

"I gained from the lady professor (married) assurances of the refining influences of 'coeducation' on both male and female students. No scandal had ever been heard of. The young ladies had weekly receptions in their separate residence building, and I had the good fortune to be present at one of them. There was excellent music and theatricals, and the presence of the professors did not interfere with the freedom and enjoyment of the young people.

"Next morning (Sunday) I heard an eloquent discourse by President Mann in the college chapel, and excellent music from a well-trained choir of students."

President and Mrs. Mann, Conway said, "felt profoundly their responsibility for the success of this experiment in coeducation. . . ."

"Coeducation at Antioch had not grown out of any theory. The plain western farmers wished their sons and daughters to have a good education without sending them

[*176*]

East; the various communities wished to obtain good teachers, male and female, without getting them at heavy cost from regions unacquainted with their conditions. That tall slender Horace Mann, with his pure, intellectual face beneath its crown of white hair, was steadily giving his heart's blood to achieve a final triumph for American education. . . ."

From the knowledge he had gained of education both at home and abroad while he was Secretary of the Massachusetts Board of Education, Mann had clear ideas of what he intended to have taught at Antioch. "I want to transfer the more improved methods of instruction and discipline and the advanced ideas of education from the East to the West."

He favored science over the classics, although the classics were offered: the Antioch curriculum carried courses in botany, physical geography, chemistry, zoology, natural philosophy (physics), civil engineering, astronomy, geology, and mineralogy as well as Latin and Greek and literature. Both French and German were also taught, as were a number of courses in mathematics and history.

At a time when almost no attention was given to health education, Mann introduced a course in human physiology and hygiene. He had learned much from George Combe, and he intended to pass what he had learned on to younger people. "Every day we have a bell rung," he reported to Samuel Howe, "and Professors and other teachers meet the whole body of pupils for exercise," which, of course, was always conducted with windows opened or, in good weather, on the campus. Every person should exercise to the point of free perspiration every day, he said. He set an example for his students and faculty by hoeing in his garden and chopping wood. The latter activity, he observed, warmed him twice.

The seniors had no elective courses; all other classes had a number of them. But the seniors had to take the required course, which covered political economy, constitutional law, evidences of Christianity, natural theology, and moral philosophy (ethics), all taught by Mann. At that time it was the usual practice for the president of a college to teach natural theology, because most of the college presidents of the day were clergymen. Mann took much pleasure in the thought that he was probably the first college president in the West who was not a clergyman.

The core of the Antioch educational system was, of course, the teachers. The students were important to Horace Mann; but he would not have been true to his background and his beliefs if he had not concentrated his greatest hopes and most passionate attention upon the members of the teaching faculty. Everything he had learned over the years about education and teaching methods he passed along to them.

He wrote to the Reverend Samuel J. May, the former principal of the normal school at Lexington, in 1858: "All of our faculty now, except myself, are young (and I feel so) and are all well qualified for their places, and filled with a generous enthusiasm. Five of them are members of the Christian church, two of the Unitarian church. Two of our professors are ladies."

He believed that the teaching at Antioch was superior: "We have the testimony of all our most intelligent students, that they have never *felt* such teaching before."

But good or great though the teachers were, none could thrill the students as could Mann himself.

[*178*]

"His mode of teaching was suggestive and stimulating," one of his students told the audience at Antioch's 1860 Commencement. He did not so much hold "his flock to the dusty, travel-worn path as to forbid their free access to every inviting meadow or spring by the way. It was his wont to hear us recite a few hours each week, assigning special lessons to special pupils, giving each some question, some theory, some matter-of-fact inquiry, on which each should pursue investigation at leisure, and prepare a paper to be read before the whole class, and be commented upon by himself. The range of these topics (when political economy was the subject)—taking in questions of agriculture and soil-fertilization, of canals and railroads, of commerce, of cotton gins, of steam plows, of population, of schools, of churches and public charities in their economic relations, and of those rising civilizations which bear on art and foster science—illustrates the comprehensiveness of Mr. Mann's favorite methods of educating and instructing our minds."

Mann imparted a certain personal impulse to all of his students, this young man said. Mann's mind "smote" their minds, "rousing us, and kindling a heat of enthusiasm. . . . It was in this that he was so incomparable. A man might as well hope to dwell under the sun unmoved, as not to glow when brought to feel his fervid love of truth. . . . The fresh delight of childhood seemed miraculously prolonged through his life; truth never palled upon his mind; the world of thought never wore a sickly light. . . ."

The stream of famous visitors who came to Yellow Springs because of the Manns' presence there was an education in itself. Julia and Samuel Howe visited there. The Manns, Julia said, "almost ate us up, so glad were they to see us." Senator Charles Sumner came, too, even though he had not approved of Mann's leaving Massachusetts. Governor Salmon P. Chase of Ohio; Miss Elizabeth Peabody; the famous Unitarian minister, John Pierpont; Josiah Quincy, Jr., the Boston writer; Bayard Taylor, renowned poet and journalist; and Horace Greeley, editor of the New York *Tribune*, visited Mann and gave lectures. Mann invited Theodore Parker to give a lecture, also, but Parker declined, although he visited Mann: ". . . it would be improper for such a heretic as I am to preach at Antioch on Sunday. . . . I wish to know if there is not some place in its neighborhood, say Dayton, where so wicked a man could hold forth and be welcome. . . ."

An estimate of Antioch's high academic standards was given by George L. Cary, a Harvard graduate who taught under Mann and later was president of Meadville Theological Seminary: "The methods of instruction adopted could not be distinguished from those in use in Harvard or Yale, and the first class graduated could hardly have been subjected to stricter examinations at either of these universities."

In May of 1856, Mann sat down to write to his old friend, George Combe: "Our college is most prosperous in all respects but the want of money."

Chapter *15*

A Victory for Humanity

Antioch College was no garden of Eden. In Eden financial
worries and sectarian difficulties were unknown. Antioch,
from the beginning, had both.

Austin Craig—who became one of Mann's dearest
friends, a professor at Antioch for a time, and eventually one
of Antioch's presidents—had been too optimistic when he
wrote Mann that money would be forthcoming for the young
college. Mann and Judge Mills had been too optimistic. In
August of 1858, five years after Antioch was opened, Mann
wrote an accurate evaluation of the financial situation: "In
all institutions like ours, there must be two departments,—
the educational and the financial. In ours, the educational
has prospered beyond any thing that I have ever known or
heard of. The financial has been as disastrous as it could be.
. . . The college was bankrupt on the day it opened—miser-
ably bankrupt."

Austin Craig had also been too idealistic when he presented Mann with the picture of the Christian denomination's beliefs. He had said in all honesty, because he was a
member of the Christian Church and these were his beliefs:

"The Bible is our rule to the exclusion of all creeds, covenants, disciplines and articles of faith ever prepared by uninspired men and imposed upon the church."

By 1857, Mann was writing, "When I came [to Antioch], I soon found that I was never among a more sectarian people in my life than no inconsequential number of these were. The whole interest which some of them manifested in the school was, whether I would say their religious *hic, haec, hoc* after them."

There had been misunderstandings all the way around. Mann had believed something he wanted to believe about a liberal religious faith and a liberal institution of higher learning. The delegates' decision to found a college that would afford equal educational opportunities to both sexes (and, as it turned out, to all races) and without sectarian bias had won him unconditionally to the cause of Antioch College. The fame of Horace Mann as an educator had won the delegates unconditionally to him as the College's first president. The noblest motives had brought about a unity that was truly there at first, but could not last. The differences were too great.

At a time when almost every college in the country had church sponsorship of one sort or another and when required chapel was the rule, the Christians were brought into line by social pressure. They did not want their college to be called atheistic, ungodly, as it was being called. To them, Mann seemed to be favoring what they considered the overly liberal beliefs of the Unitarians in faculty, in textbooks, in a whole way of life. The leaders of the Christian denomination, for Mann's part, seemed not to be living up to their pledge when they tried to insist upon required chapel. As an earnest of his belief in the good faith of the Christians, he joined the Christian Church in Yellow Springs—and Mary Mann and Rebecca Pennell joined with him—but he would not have required chapel. People must be religious inside themselves, he thought, not because religion was imposed upon them.

In any case, the Christians lacked "experience in financing a great institution."

The towers were there at Antioch. The ideals were there. The educational program was there. But there was no money.

"I have done everything for Antioch," Mann said, "except praise it and beg money for it."

Yet praise it he did. He could not resist setting down his pride in it. "This is the only liberal institution of a first-class character for more than six millions of population," he wrote. "Such a field is here ready as the angel of the Lord never yet put sickle into it."

And beg money for it, he did. He gave the College more money than he ever received in salary. He went on lecture tours to raise money for it. To Downer, who invested what funds Mann had from the sale of his West Newton home and to whom Mann could always speak frankly, he wrote in 1857: " . . . I am living on short allowance; have not had a cent from the college for a year and a half; and it costs me about $2,000 a year to keep up my 'public house.' " He and Calvin Pennell, he wrote, could give their services without charge. " . . . But we cannot pluck Antioch College from the abyss into which it threatens to fall."

He asked his friends to help raise money, also. Samuel Howe reported that he had not been very successful in getting contributions, because a number of people would never forgive Mann for "assailing their Fetish," that is, Daniel Webster.

From the beginning, the Unitarians had interested themselves in Antioch. Their interest was selfless. They wanted to see a nonsectarian college not only survive but grow strong, able to stand as an example of how truly great a nonsectarian college could be. They wanted to open up nonsectarian education for the West. As early as December of 1853, the Unitarian *Christian Register* began soliciting contributions for Antioch. Two Unitarian groups visited the College in 1854 to inspect it. These visits resulted in call after call to Unitarian groups across the country for contributions to the College. At All Souls Church in New York, $25,000 in contributions was raised. Dr. George Washington Hosmer of Buffalo, later to become another of Antioch's presidents, made special pleas. President Stebbins of the Meadville Theological School in Pennsylvania took to the road on behalf of Antioch. Meadville had been organized in 1844 by Christians and Unitarians for the training of their ministers, but the Christians had withdrawn from the endeavour in 1848.

From Meadville, Stebbins wrote to Mann, "Our best success here, depends on your success there." At another time he wrote, "The desperate fight at Thermopylae was nothing compared with your struggle to save Antioch from its debts."

Again and again the Unitarians came to the rescue of the small college, and almost succeeded in paying off its debts. In the academic year of 1858-59, however, the College's expenses were far greater than income, because all large contributions were going toward paying off debts. Horace

[184]

Mann said, "Internally the establishment goes on beautifully, but already the trump of doom is sounding in our ears and the college is to be offered for sale."

This was what every one had been dreading. The Presbyterians and Catholics were rumored to be planning to bid on the property. If an orthodox sect purchased it, nonsectarian education might be forever dead in the West.

The College was declared bankrupt, and the buildings and land of Antioch were put up at auction in Cincinnati in April of 1859. Horace Mann, Eli Fay, and a group of Christian and Unitarian friends pooled their personal resources and bought it back for $40,200. A Christian journal commented editorially, "The world is almost without a parallel in the disinterestedness of their [the Unitarians'] liberality shown toward the Christians in the final rescue of Antioch College."

Antioch was saved!

The significance of the event can be measured by words Mann had spoken many years before. The public schools were his song, he said, but the song was not yet ended: "We're still dependent on the orthodox college for our leadership. We carry our children through the grades democratically, and then if they go on to college they go back again to the drag chain of creeds, and discrimination against women, sect, race, and color. We must have colleges which are free, or our system will be defenseless from the start."

Commencement of 1859 was an exalted occasion. Mann had been up since early in the morning finishing his speech, which he still had not had time to read over before he rose to address the graduates and guests. He was so moved that he found it difficult to speak. He knew what those young men

"I feel few doubts that you will be greater...."

and women before him had been suffering in their worries
for him and for the College. He remembered what they had
all shared together over the last four years. He said:

"I wonder how far we have come, as yet, with education.
I wonder how many we have taken from the one side, and
given to the other. That is very important to me. In a way,
the success or failure of my own life depends on how many of
you pass from one side to the other.

"And yet as I see you, as I look in your faces, and as I
recall you as you came here, and as I recall the things that

have passed between us, I feel few doubts that you will be greater, ay, much greater, than those of us who came before you. . . .

"This is Antioch College still, the same as we have known and loved heretofore; but, according to the doctrine of metempsychosis, it is by the transmigration of the old soul into a new body. The old body, with its works (that is, its scholarships and debts, its promises to pay without paying, and its vestments of liberty without liberty) is dead; and in its stead we have the resurrection of a new and glorified body. . . .

"This beneficent change has not been accomplished without a great struggle. . . .

"And so, young ladies and gentlemen of the graduating class, after journeying together for so many years on our passage through life, we are about to part. Another day, ay, another hour, and we separate. Would to God I could continue this journey with you through all its future course! I cannot go with you. . . .

"But I can enshrine my spirit in your hearts, so that when I fall in the ranks, you may pursue the conflict and win the victory. . . .

"Let me sum up all I have said in a paragraph.

"In the infinitely noble battle in which you are engaged against error and wrong, if ever repulsed or stricken down, may you always be solaced and cheered by the exulting cry of triumph over some abuse in Church or State, some vice or folly in society, some false opinion or cruelty or guilt which you have overcome! And I beseech you to treasure up in your hearts these, my parting words: *Be ashamed to die until you have won some victory for humanity.*"

[*187*]

Mann was described at that Commencement as looking "too happy, but very tired."

Yes, Antioch was saved. But Horace Mann was 63 years of age, he had been through a great struggle, and he was very tired.

The next day, Mary Mann said, he was nearly speechless with fatigue. He still had before him a two-day committee meeting. There seemed no place that he could turn for rest. It was hot and dry that summer. The Ohio cornfields and the lawns of Yellow Springs were parched and burned. The leaves on the trees gave only a dry rustle in the hot wind.

Mann wandered around the house, stretching out, "now on the sofa, now on the floors, praying for rain, mourning over the time he was losing for preparation of duties to come, but conscious only of suffering, not of near death."

He asked Georgie to hum for him. He wanted no other sound, and only interrupted George once when he heard a few rain drops falling on the tin roof of the piazza. "Stop a minute," he said, "and let me listen to that music!"

He was now very ill with what physicians diagnosed as milk sickness, a kind of malignant fever. He could eat nothing. Mary and the two younger boys were ill, too (young Horace was in the East); but Mary was with him whenever she could be. Rebecca Pennell and Eli Fay were there, and "relays of devoted students brought him fresh draughts every hour from the only cool well in the neighborhood." Dr. Pulte was summoned from Cincinnati.

Mann was finally told he had but three hours to live. "I do not feel it to be so," he replied, "but, if it is so, I have something to say."

He asked to see those of his students who were still in

Yellow Springs; and one by one they came to him, and he talked with them for the last time about their problems and their lives.

At last he said, "I should like to have Mr. Fay make a short prayer, low, peaceful, grateful!"

He dictated affectionate messages to be sent to his loved ones who were absent—young Horace, his sister, Mr. Craig, and other old friends. "And those good young men, Mr. Fay, who have always done their duty—how I love them. Tell them how I love them." From time to time he cried out, almost in delirium, "Oh, my beautiful plans for the college!"

At last he asked for quiet, and said, "Will not the friends fall back?"

"I can sleep now, if there is no noise." To Mary, he said, "Sing to me, if you have the heart."

"Yes," she said, and sang something without words. Later she would break down. Later she would grieve. But as long as Horace Mann needed her, she would be there to do as he asked.

Horace Mann died on August 2, 1859. He was temporarily buried on the Antioch College campus, where a stone shaft now marks the place. On the simple monument are engraved the words, "And I beseech you to treasure up in your hearts these, my parting words: Be ashamed to die until you have won some victory for humanity." Antioch students today sit on the mound and lean against the shaft, sometimes with books open before them, sometimes just dreaming in the sunlight.

Mary Mann broke up the household and took the boys East—at first to Wayside in Concord, which Sophia Hawthorne had offered as shelter. Mary brought her husband's

[*189*]

body East to Providence, where she carried out an agreement she and Horace Mann had made long before. His grave is between Charlotte's and Mary's, and on his monument are the words:

What is excellent, as God lives, is permanent.
Hearts are dust, hearts' loves remain;
Heart's love will meet thee again.

Mary educated the boys, wrote and edited an invaluable *Life and Works of Horace Mann,* and again went into a teaching partnership with Elizabeth.

Samuel Howe raised money—a considerable amount of it in pennies from Massachusetts school children—and a statue of Horace Mann was erected on the Massachusetts State House lawn facing a statue of Daniel Webster. A replica of the statue stands on the highest point of Antioch's Glen Helen, facing the Main Hall towers.

Mann's writings have been translated into many languages, and biographies about him have been written in several. School houses all over the world are named for him. On Mann's tablet in the Hall of Fame are the words from one of his statements: "The Common School is the greatest discovery ever made by man. . . . "

But Mann's life is his monument. He knew that he would not see all his ideals realized during his lifetime. He wrote to Samuel Howe: "We must draw our encouragement more from our faith and our philosophy than from realization." He said to Theodore Parker that his labors and sacrifices at Antioch would not be productive until after he had been removed from the scene.

He also said, "The idea of vindicating one spot of freedom of opinion and freedom of inquiry, and hallowing it to the living spirit of a sectional Christianity, seemed to me sufficient to make a man leave home and friends to consecrate his life to the work."

Wherever men believe in freedom and justice and equal opportunity for all, the spirit of Horace Mann rises and gives them renewed strength to carry on the fight against ignorance.

ACKNOWLEDGMENTS

Credit for much in this book should go to the late Robert L. Straker, Antioch '25, who spent more than 20 years amassing a vast collection of notes, letters and documents related to Mann, which he left to the Massachusetts Historical Society and to Antioch College; and to Miss Bessie L. Totten, Curator Emerita of the Antiochiana Historical Collection, for invaluable help and advice. Any errors in the use of these aids are my own.

Jessie Cambron Treichler